Purich's Aboriginal Issues Series

INDIGENOUS PEOPLES OF THE WORLD

AN INTRODUCTION TO THEIR PAST, PRESENT, AND FUTURE

Brian Goehring

Purich Publishing
Saskatoon, Saskatchewan
Canada

Purich Publishing
P.O. Box 23032, Market Mall Postal Outlet
Saskatoon, SK Canada S7J 5H3

Canadian Cataloguing in Publication Data

Goehring, Elmer Brian, 1951–

Indigenous peoples of the world

(Purich's aboriginal issues series)
Includes bibliographical references and index.
ISBN 1–895830–01–X

1. Indigenous peoples. 2. Economic development - Social aspects. I. Title. II. Series.

GN380.G64 1993 305.8 C93–098149–9

Editing and text design by Jane McHughen
Cover design by Next Communications Inc., Saskatoon
Maps by Brian Goehring and Don Norris
Printed in Canada by Kromar Printing Ltd.
Printed on acid-fee paper

Readers will note that words like Aboriginal, Native, and Indigenous have been capitalized. In recent years, many Aboriginal people have argued that such words should be capitalized when referring to specific people, in the same manner that words such as European and American are capitalized. I agree; hence, the capitalization. *Donald Purich, Publisher*

TABLE OF CONTENTS

ACKNOWLEDGMENTS

The ideas and concepts in this book represent the present distillation of larger themes in the process of rapid evolution. As such, both in the larger world of concrete reality, and in my perception and synthesis thereof, this volume represents very much a report on work in progress. All responsibility for errors of interpretation, omissions or flawed philosophical constructs are mine, and mine alone. This book represents but the start of the process of beginning to understand an area of immense complexity.

I would like to acknowledge the invaluable contributions of time, effort, and energy expended on my behalf by a host of university professors in the process to date. At the University of Saskatchewan, William Barr, Robert M. Bone, and John McConnell, the remnants of the old Institute of Northern Studies, have had the patience to bear with me through several undergraduate degrees. At the University of British Columbia, Julie Cruickshank and Robin Ridington of the Department of Anthropology and Sociology, and Trevor Barnes, Chris Burn (now at Carleton), Rex Casinader, Derek Gregory, Cole Harris, David Ley, J. Ross Mackay, Gerry Pratt, Maureen Reed, J. Lewis Robinson, and Dong Ho Shin of the Department of Geography have provided stimulating and learned academic challenges and discourse over the years, and have been invaluable mentors and academic role models through the course of my graduate apprenticeship.

I would also like to acknowledge the primary role played by the members of my PhD Committee at the University of British Columbia: Paul Tennant of the Department of Political Science, and Ken Denike, Robert North, and J. K. Stager of the Department of Geography. It was this committee that first suggested that this topic be explored, and this book be written.

As a researcher, I would like to thank those agencies and institutions who have provided me with assistance and support in my ongoing studies of the economic evolution of the Kitikmeot Region of the Proposed Nunavut Territory. These include the Northern Scientific Training Program of the Arctic and Alpine Committee of the University of British Columbia, the Government of the Northwest Territories, First Air Ltd., and especially Mr. Doug Willy and the management of Echo Bay Mines Ltd.

I have spent, and continue to spend, time in and about the Inuit world.

Acknowledgments

Within this world, I would like to express gratitude to those who have assisted me greatly over the years. First and foremost, I should like to acknowledge a debt of gratitude to Mr. David Katik, now deceased, and his family of Coppermine. David spent years taking me out hunting or fishing on the land nearly every weekend and holiday. He introduced me to the arcane arts of Inuit snowmobile and outboard engine repair alfresco, and to the skills of the land he loved. He taught me a new way to see, the essence of the Arctic as a friendly environment.

I would also like to acknowledge a debt to the elders of Pelly Bay, who articulated their world to me in past projects, and to Eric Oogark, my research assistant and translator through this work. I consider Pelly Bay as one of the jewels of the Arctic: my family and I would like to thank all of its residents for many kindnesses received during our years spent living there.

I would also like to thank those many people who have provided assistance over the years, and kindly invited me into their homes throughout the Arctic while I was travelling. These include Paul Therriault of Inuvik, Jacqueline Beland and Paul Bennett of Coppermine, Earl Laliberte, Atima Hadlari, and Kane and Elik Tologanak of Cambridge Bay, Sean Sweet of Gjoa Haven, Makabe and Dolorossa Nartok, John and Celine Ningark, and Barnaby Immingark of Pelly Bay, Millie Pigalak and Simon Kuliktana of Taloyoak, and Bonnie Howard of Iqaluit.

As well, I would express a debt of gratitude to the officers and staff members of the Kitikmeot Inuit Association, the Tunguvut Federation of Nunavut, and the Kitimeot Hamlet Councils, who have provided me with invaluable assistance in my research endeavours. I also wish to acknowledge the kind efforts and assistance of Donald Purich and Jane McHughen in the editing and revising of this volume, and of Purich Publishing for its ultimate publication.

Finally, I would like to acknowledge the gracious and continuing support of my wife, Myrna Ziola, who works at a real job to support me and my family while I am engaged in the academic enterprises of my Doctoral apprenticeship, and which has allowed me the financial and academic freedom to write this book.

Figure I: Indigenous Peoples of the World

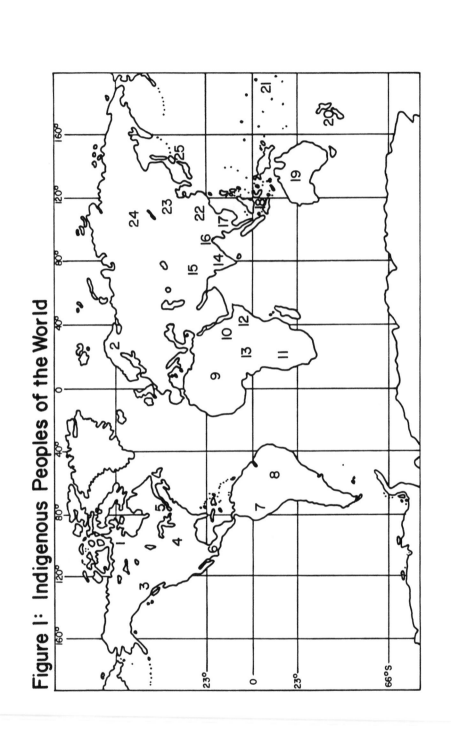

FIGURE 1: INDIGENOUS PEOPLES OF THE WORLD

1. INUIT

2. SAMI

3. NORTH AMERICAN PACIFIC COAST PEOPLES, includes Cowichan, Gitskan, Haida, Haisla, Heiltsuk, Klamath, Klukwan, Kwagiulth, Nisga'a, Nuu'chah'nulth, Nuxalk, Sechelt, Squamish, Sto:lo, Tlingit, Tsimshian, Yakima

4. MOUNTAIN, PLAINS, AND INTERIOR WOODLANDS PEOPLES OF NORTH AMERICA, includes Apache, Arapaho, Cherokee, Cheyenne, Chipewyan, Comanche, Cree, Crow, Blackfoot, Dene, Hopi, Innu, Iowa, Keres, Kiowa, Métis, Navajo, Nez Perce, Omaha, Paiute, Pawnee, Pueblo, Shawnee, Shoshone, Sioux, Uti, Winnebago, Wintu

5. EASTERN WOODLANDS AND COASTAL PEOPLES OF NORTH AMERICA, includes Catawba, Cayuga, Chickahominy, Choctaw, Creek, Lumnee, Malecite, Micmac, Miccosukee, Mohegan, Mohawk, Narraganset, Oneida, Onondaga, Ottawa, Passamaquoddy, Pequet, Seminole, Seneca, Shinecock, Tuscarora, Wanpanoag

6. INDIAN PEOPLES OF MEXICO AND CENTRAL AMERICA, Maya and Aztec descendants, including Boruca, Bribari, Choco, Chol, Chorti, Chuj, Embera, Guatuso, Guami, Huichol, Kekchi, Kuna, Lacandon, Lenca, Miskito, Mixe, Nahua, Pepile, Quiche, Rama, Sumu, Tarahumara, Yaqui, Yucatec, Zapotec

7. HIGHLAND AND MOUNTAIN PEOPLES OF SOUTH AMERICA, includes Inca descendants, Aguaruna, Ashanika, Aymara, Ayoreo, Cauca, Chiraguano, Chiquitano, Cofan, Colorado Pinchada, Garavo, Matsigenka, Mojo, Otavala, Quechua, Shuar, Siona, Waorani

8. LOWLAND PEOPLES OF SOUTH AMERICA, includes Ache, Aquaruna, Akawaio, Amarakaeri, Amehusha, Aracanian, Arara, Arawak, Arawete, Ashaninka, Asurini, Bari, Embera, Gaviao, Guahibo, Guajiro, Guambiano, Guarani, Itaipu, Kalinja, Kayapo, Kolla, Kreen-Akrore, Lakono, Makuxi, Mapuche, Mataco, Matsigenk, Nambikwara, Paez, Panare, Parakana, Pataxo-Ho-Hoe, Piaroa, Sanema, Shipibo, Toba, Tucuri, Tukano, Txukurromae, Ufaina, Waimititi-Aitroari, Waorani, Wayana, Xavante, Yagua, Yanesh, Yanomami

9. SAHEL AND SAHARAN PEOPLES: Tuareg, Fulani

10. PASTORAL PEOPLES OF EAST AFRICA: Dinka, Fipa, Hadzabe, Masai, Nuer, Oromo

11. HUNTER AND GATHERERS OF SOUTHERN AFRICA: Kung(san), Twa, Zhutwasi

12. INDIGENOUS PEOPLES OF THE HORN OF AFRICA: Eritrean, Somali, Tigrayan

13. RAINFOREST PEOPLES OF AFRICA: Bantu, Efe, Lese, Mbuli (Pygmies), Mbuti

14. SCHEDULED TRIBES OF INDIA AND SRI LANKA, includes Andamese, Bhil, Bhilala, Chencha, Dandami, Garo, Gond, Ho Inula Karumbas, Juangs, Kadras, Kameng, Khasi, Khond, Kolha, Korku, Lohit, Malaipantram, Manipuri, Mizo, Munda, Naga, Oroan, Ratra, Santal, Saveras, Shobgas, Tadari, Todakotas, Vasari, Vedda

15. MOUNTAIN PEOPLES OF CENTRAL ASIA, includes Afghan, Baluch, Kurds, Pathan

16. HILL TRIBES, includes Akha, Arakenese, Bunjugi, Chakma, Chin, Hmong, Kachin, Karen Khumi, Khyang, Lahu, Lisu, Lushai, Marma, Mro, Murong, Pankhu, Paluang, Shan, Tripura, Yao

17. INDIGENOUS PEOPLES OF SOUTHEAST ASIA, includes Iban, Javai, Kayan, Meo, Momtagnards, Negritos, Penan, Songoi

18. SOUTHEAST ASIAN ISLAND PEOPLES, includes Amungme, Asmat, Bontoc, Chimbo, Dani, Dayak, Huli, Iban, Isneg, Kapaku, Kayan, Kedang, Kelabit, Kenyah, Kha Htin, Kha Mu, Kyaka, Lawa, Mae-Enga, Mangyan, Manobo, Maranao, Melpa, Tsembaga, Tausag, Yakan

19. ABORIGINAL PEOPLES OF AUSTRALIA, includes Gurindji, Kokotha, Manjiljara, Pitjan-tatjara, Torres Straight Islanders, Yrrkla, Yungera

20. MAORI OF AOTEARORA (New Zealand)

21. POLYNESIAN AND MELANESIAN PEOPLES OF THE PACIFIC ISLANDS, includes Chamorro, Fijian, Hawaiian, Kanaky, Samoan, Solomon Islanders, Tahitian, Tongan, Vanua

22. NATIONAL MINORITIES OF CHINA, many groups, 55 recognized. The largest include Bai, Bouyei, Dong, Hani, Hui, Manchu, Miao, Mongol, Tibetan, Tujia, Uygur, Yao, Yi

23. MONGOL PEOPLES

24. "SMALL PEOPLES" OF RUSSIA AND THE FORMER USSR, includes Aluet, Altay Kizhi, Ainu, Buryat, Chelkantsy, Chulyman, Chukchi, Chukots, Dolgan, Entsy, Even, Evenk, Itel'meny, Kety, Khakash, Khanty, Koryaki, Kumandintsy, Mansi, Nanaytsy, Negidaltsy, Nenetsy, Nganasan, Nivkhi, Olofan, Orok, Samigiry, Sel'kupy, Shortsky, Tatar, Teleky, Tolofari, Tubalari, Tuvintsy, Udegey, Ul'chi, Yakutsk, Yakugir

25. AINU OF JAPAN

Figure 2 : World Distribution : Indigenous Peoples

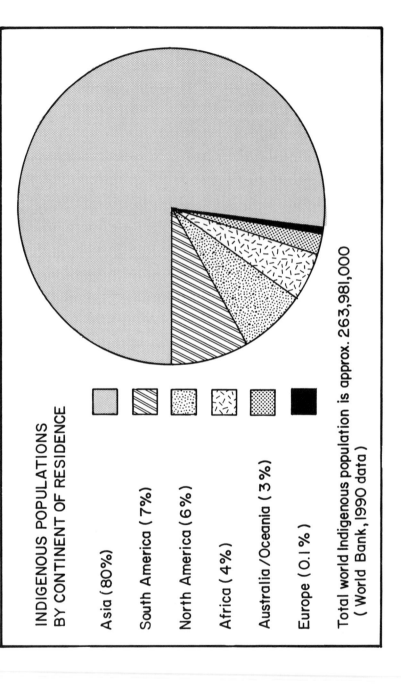

INDIGENOUS POPULATIONS
BY CONTINENT OF RESIDENCE

Asia (80%)

South America (7%)

North America (6%)

Africa (4%)

Australia /Oceania (3%)

Europe (0.1%)

Total world Indigenous population is approx. 263,981,000
(World Bank,1990 data)

Figure 3: Nations With Indigenous Majority Population

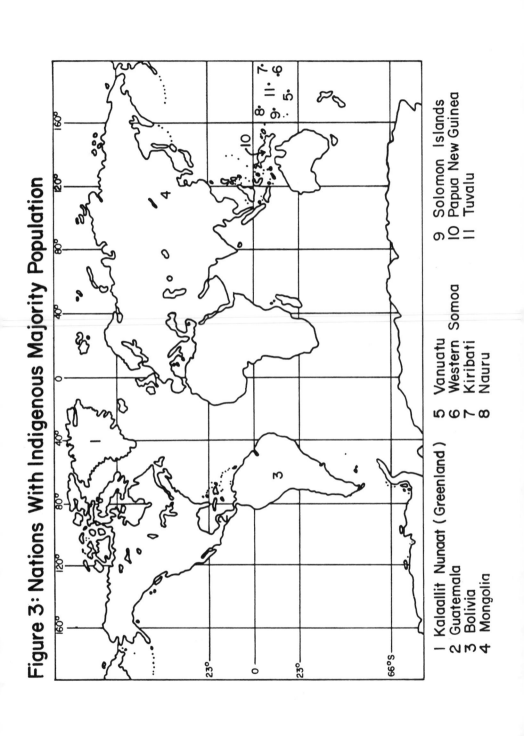

1 Kalaallit Nunaat (Greenland)
2 Guatemala
3 Bolivia
4 Mongolia

5 Vanuatu
6 Western Somoa
7 Kiribati
8 Nauru

9 Solomon Islands
10 Papua New Guinea
11 Tuvalu

Figure 4: Nations With Indigenous Populations Over 1 Million

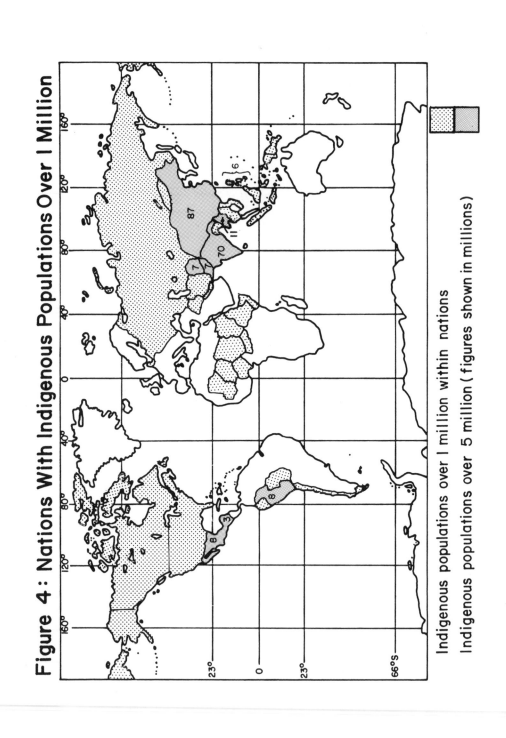

Indigenous populations over 1 million within nations

Indigenous populations over 5 million (figures shown in millions)

Figure 5: Remaining Frontier Areas of the World Today

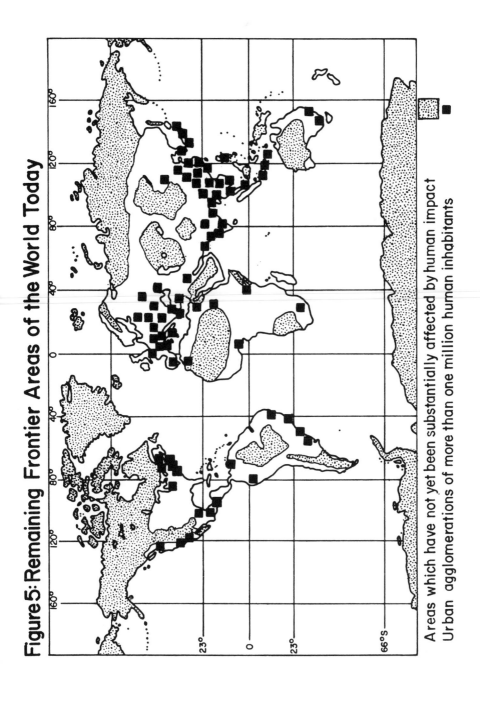

Areas which have not yet been substantially affected by human impact

Urban agglomerations of more than one million human inhabitants

Figure 6 : Indigenous Peoples : Present Land Use Practices

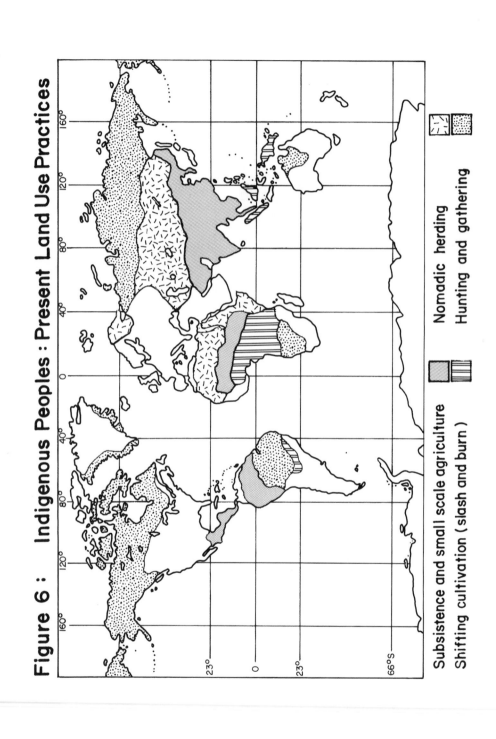

Subsistence and small scale agriculture

Shifting cultivation (slash and burn)

Nomadic herding

Hunting and gathering

CHAPTER 1

BACKGROUND

INTRODUCTION

If economy is taken to mean the whole way of life of a people—the ways in which they wrest a livelihood from the environment in which they live—then the economies of all Indigenous Peoples of the world have been forced through a series of massive changes as a result of uninvited and overriding contact with the now-dominant Eurocentric world economy.

From its origins in seventeenth-century England, industrial capitalism has grown to encompass the entire planet. The majority of the inhabitants of the world today hold a critical stake in the continued existence of the capitalist economic order, as we become citizens of a world linked by common economic ties. By early next century more people will be urban and industrialized than will be rural, tribal, and reliant upon traditional economies. This expansionist form of economic organization, and its allied ethic of "modernity," has grown to become dominant by its very nature: it must expand in order to survive.

The phenomenal growth of the global capitalist economy has had a great impact upon the economic organizations developed by Indigenous Peoples of the world. This impact can be summarized in three general terms: contact, conflict, and crisis. There are certain similarities between Indigenous economies, and when faced with common experiences of contact with the monolith of modernity, their reactions of conflict and crisis have been, in many instances, comparable.

This work analyzes, in broad general strokes, the effects that rapid expansion of the unilaterally imposed economic paradigm of modernity has had upon Indigenous Peoples of the world and on their economies. It unifies similar strands of experience worldwide into several synthesized themes of the past, present, and future.

As all economies begin to become inexorably linked into the universalist global village, a process of basic redefinition of the nature and extent of preexisting paradigms and philosophies is being forced upon Indigenous Peoples worldwide. Worldviews that once extended only to the next

1

valley are being expanded to a planetary perspective. Inherently holistic and all-encompassing traditional tribal philosophical perceptions and perspectives, lifeworlds that once served to connect cause and effect in a culturally acceptable manner, fail in many ways to explain present concepts of reality.

There are great holes in many Indigenous perceptual realities today, as the economic and philosophical underpinnings that had served their ancestors falter or fall in the face of overwhelming changes introduced into their traditional territories. South America's Yanomamo society has met the might of capitalism, and will never be the same again. Isolated African tribespeople who eke a living from hunting and gathering or slash-and-burn agriculture in the way of their ancestors now line the streets to welcome Michael Jackson to their villages. Arctic Inuit pause to have coffee and change country-and-western tapes in their portable cassette players while seal hunting on the sea ice, and return to ranch-style bungalows in permanent settlements to watch hockey games or kung-fu videos on television screens. Indigenous People the world over are in a process of redefinition, as they attempt to rediscover and reinvent their relationships to a radically changed environment not entirely of their own making.

As the perceptual confines of the planet have shrunk, it is the Indigenous Peoples and economies of the world that have had to face the most overwhelming changes and make the most radical adjustments. It has been their societies that have borne the brunt of the displacement necessary to establish the present global economic order. In many areas Indigenous Peoples now find the basic rules of existence have been altered without their knowledge. They have lost their fundamental sense of direction in a world gone awry, which they had once understood in its entirety. As Indigenous Peoples struggle to find their way in the new order, their very existence as peoples is being challenged.

Yet the one thing that has allowed for the continued existence of Indigenous Peoples worldwide is their resilience. Indigenous Peoples will continue to exist, will continue to avoid assimilation into the mainstreams of their national economies, and, through adaptation, will emerge through the present periods of contact, conflict, and crisis to survive altered but partially intact. In many areas of the world the fundamental injustices of the past are now being critically reexamined. New and vibrant Indigenous organizations, effectively utilizing political, economic, and perceptual tools unrecognizable to their ancestors, yet adapted and attuned to the realities of the new world order, are achieving reconciliation with modernity as modernity is adjusting to allow for the presence of new voices within it. Worldwide, Indigenous Peoples are now attempting to define the changes that have affected their lives. The historical processes of the past are interpreted by the realities of the present to formulate the perceptual paradigms by which they will live in the future. Indigenous realities are in the process of being reinvented today.

DEFINITIONS

Within the tangled and often murky interpretations of the past it is sometimes difficult to reconstruct a people's relationship with the land from which they once derived a livelihood. Historical and contemporary oral recordings of the past attest to great migrations and displacements of peoples over time, and these movements continue on a large scale to the present day. In many cases it is difficult to reconstruct these movements and to determine who lived where, when, and for how long.

Added to the difficulty of establishing the historical record with any degree of certainty is the problem of defining perceptual boundaries. Within today's world of legally defined, finite, and defended borders it is difficult to imagine a time without precise delineations of territorial ownership. Yet this has been the case for most of humankind's tenure upon the planet. In the preindustrial past there have been times and places where borders were largely irrelevant. In some cases the concept of borders was beyond a society's conception. The Thule Inuit of northeast Greenland (Kalaallit Nunaat) until recently believed that they were the only people to inhabit the earth. The entire earth was theirs, in their perception, to far beyond where they could possibly travel.

Today's arbitrary, linear, and infinitely definable borders, in a world in which there are complex legal arguments mounted over square meters of surface ownership, are an historical anomaly. For most of our existence on this planet, borders, when they existed at all, were vague constructs and were perceptually rather ill defined. In many instances natural delineations sufficed; in other cases there were seasonal or long-term land-use overlaps, as with the Dene and Inuit of northern North America, who shared territory in opposing seasons about the tree-line margins. A great deal of fluidity and nebulousness could prevail without conflicts developing. Oftentimes, borders existed solely in the minds of the peoples living at or near the margins of their perceptual realms.

3

For preindustrial peoples with little or no concept of private ownership of property, the definition of arbitrary borders to the land was not important. It is only in recent years, with the ascendancy of the Eurocentric concepts of private ownership and national sovereignty, that the need for arbitrary definition of exact borders has created conflicts. The resolutions of many of these conflicts over perceptual borders are still pending.

As well as delineating borders, there is also the semantic problem of the precise identification of Indigenous Peoples of the world. Although Indigenous Peoples themselves know who they are, the legal strictures of the postindustrial world require formal definitions, which are difficult to formulate: a quantitative society has great difficulty in defining qualitative concepts and anomalies are difficult to conceptualize.

Thus we have within Canada, for example, a situation of legal and semantic absurdity in which Ovide Mercredi, the Grand Chief of the Assembly of First Nations, was declared by an appointed panel of paternalistic non-Indigenous government bureaucrats to be legally Indigenous one month before his election to office in 1991. His daughter is not an Indian (Gillmor, 1992).

A number of terms have been used by industrial societies to refer to preexisting peoples. Many are place-specific and reflect common usage over time. Such terms as Indian, Eskimo, Aborigine, Indio, Adivasis, Orang Asli, Junglis, and Scheduled Tribes are essentially Aryan in origin, are culture-specific, and are generally not used by Indigenous Peoples to refer to themselves. In many cases there are derogatory or pejorative connotations associated with these epithets.

Several generally accepted and non-derogatory terms have emerged over the years to refer to preexisting peoples around the world. Such synonyms as Native Peoples, Autochthonous Peoples, Tribal Minorities, and National Minorities are commonly viewed today as being politically correct. In recent years the terms First Nations, Native Nations, or Founding Nations have gained increasing acceptance among many Indigenous groups as they attempt to define themselves semantically to the dominant societies in which they live.

Indigenous Peoples often resent having to define themselves to an outside society whom they view essentially as intruders. From their perspective as First Peoples, it is derogatory to be referred to as minorities in their original land. In this regard, many First Nations continue to view themselves as the continuing possessors of sovereignty at the center of a finite perceptual world. All others within this world are merely recently arrived aliens.

4

Background

At the International Non-Governmental Organizations Conference on Indigenous Peoples and the Land, sponsored by the United Nations and held in Geneva, Switzerland, September 15–18, 1981, the term Fourth World was proposed to describe the situations in which Indigenous Peoples find themselves in most countries today (Burger, 1987, p. 178). Over time this term has gained general acceptance within the academic community, but its original semantic intentions have been somewhat lessened by authors who have usurped its use to describe conditions in the sprawling slums on the margins of major third world cities.

In general, the term Indigenous Populations has emerged as the most acceptable descriptor available. A report presented to a United Nations body has even proposed a definition of Indigenous Populations that has been used by a United Nations group in its work. In 1982, the United Nations Economic and Social Council, Commission on Human Rights, adopted the following definition:

> Indigenous Populations are composed of the existing descendants of the peoples who inhabited the present territory of a country wholly or partially at the time when persons of a different culture or ethnic origin arrived there from other parts of the world, overcame them and, by conquest, settlement or other means, reduced them to a non-dominant or colonial situation; who today live more in conformity with their particular social, economic and cultural customs and traditions than with the institutions of the country of which they now form a part, under a state structure that incorporates mainly the national, social and cultural characteristics of other segments of the population that are predominant.
>
> Although they have not suffered conquest or colonization, isolated or marginal groups existing in the country should be regarded as covered by the notion of "Indigenous Populations" for the following reasons:
>
> a) they are descendants of groups which were in the territory of the country at the time when other groups of different cultures or ethnic origins arrived there;
>
> b) precisely because of their isolation from other segments of the country's population they have preserved almost intact the customs and traditions of their ancestors which are similar to those characterized as Indigenous;
>
> c) they are, even if only formally, placed under a State

structure which incorporates national, social and cultural characteristics alien to theirs (U.N., UNESCO, ref: E/Cn.4./ Sub.2/L.566, 1982).

This complex and somewhat legalistic definition has been adopted by the United Nations, and is now generally accepted worldwide. In its simplest sense, it serves to identify preexisting societies that have been overrun by global capitalism, and who have previously had a long identification with a land they considered their source of life and their birthright. Although it has its limitations, and would be challenged by some with a claim to Indigenousness, it is used to define Indigenous populations for the purposes of this examination.

WORLD DISTRIBUTION

Within the bounds of this definition, there are approximately 263,891,000 Indigenous People in the world (World Bank, 1991 data), distributed over six continents, and in more than eighty-five countries. In total they represent about 4 percent of the global population (Burger, 1990). Figure 1 illustrates the distribution of Indigenous Peoples worldwide.

By far the largest percentage of Indigenous People live in the continent of Asia (see Figure 2). China, India, and Myanmar (Burma) all have Indigenous populations over 10 million (see Figure 4). Two countries in Asia—China and India—account for nearly 60 percent of the world's Indigenous population between them. Russia east of the Ural Mountains contains at least 1 million Indigenous inhabitants of more than twenty-five distinct nationalities. In only one nation in Asia do Indigenous People form a majority. Ethnic Mongols make up approximately 90 percent of the population in Mongolia. In all other nation-states of Asia, Indigenous Peoples are minorities, comprising approximately 7.1 percent of the total population of the continent.

In Africa, 1.2 percent of the population would be considered Indigenous by the United Nations' definition. If all traditional hunting, gathering, and pastoralist people in Africa were to be included in this tabulation, the figure would rise to only 4.4 percent of the total population of the continent. If all the preexisting peoples affected by several centuries of slavery and colonialism were included, this count would increase dramatically.

Europe has by far the lowest population of Indigenous People, both in absolute numbers (80,000) and as a percentage of total population (.0002 percent). In North and South America, where once Indigenous Peoples

6

accounted for the entire population, they have now been reduced to the status of minorities in their homelands. In North America approximately 5.7 percent of the present population is of Indigenous ancestry, while in South America the figure has been reduced to 4 percent.

In Canada, the recently released results of the 1991 Census indicate an increase in the number of citizens claiming Aboriginal ancestry. Statistics Canada lists a total of 1,002,675 who claim Indigenousness, a jump of 41 percent in five years, from 2.8 percent of the population in 1986 to 3.7 percent in 1991. Much of this increase is semantic: with a rebirth of Native pride many citizens identified as non-Native in the last census have now chosen to identify officially with their Aboriginal ancestry.

In Australia, approximately 2 percent of the population is now Indigenous. In New Zealand, 10 percent of the population today is Indigenous Maori. It is only in the scattered islands of the Pacific where Indigenous Peoples have managed to retain their numerical status over a large area. If Oceania is included with Australia, approximately 25 percent of the combined population would be considered Indigenous.

It is in the Pacific that the processes of decolonization have seen the rise of a number of independent states with Indigenous majorities (see Figure 3). The small island-nations of Tonga, Vanuatu, Kiribati, Tuvalu, Western Samoa, Papua New Guinea, the Solomon Islands, and Nauru all have populations with Indigenous majorities. The colonies and protectorates of French Polynesia, Guam, and the Wallis and Futuna Islands have Indigenous majorities that are seeking to achieve greater autonomy and independence in the future. In both Fiji and New Caledonia the Indigenous Peoples fall just short of a majority, and are actively seeking to redress the demographic imbalances of recent history.

In other areas of the world there are only a very few places where Indigenous Peoples find themselves still to be a majority in their traditional homelands. The Mongol Peoples have only very recently emerged from Communist domination and are now actively pursuing their own course of self-determination. In Kalaallit Nunaat (Greenland), where Indigenous Inuit comprise 91 percent of the population, a limited form of home rule under the aegis of Denmark has been in place since 1979.

In Bolivia, where 66 percent of the population is Indigenous, and in Guatemala, where slightly more than half of the population can claim Indigenous descent, First Nation majorities have yet to translate demography into real self-determination as peoples. In both of these countries the Indigenous Peoples have been and continue to be subjugated to the political and economic domination of the ruling minorities.

7

In most areas of the world the artificial, Eurocentric borders of the past remain in place to define the bounds of the nation-states of today. Imposed during the eras of colonial expansion, most of these national borders do not reflect in any manner the ethnic composition and the traditional territories of the preexisting peoples. Many Indigenous Peoples now find themselves living across several arbitrarily imposed borders, spread throughout larger and alien nations. In North America, several First Nations, such as the Mohawk and Blackfoot, exist across the Canada-U.S. border. Ethnic Mongols live across three nations of Asia, while Kurdish Peoples are spread throughout four. The Sami of Europe exist across four national jurisdictions (Finland, Sweden, Norway, and Russia), while in Africa the Indigenous Tuareg exist across five other nations, and the Fulani across eight. In many cases this cross-border distribution has weakened their political effectiveness.

As the postwar era of decolonization wanes, many peoples who consider themselves to be "nations" within the borders of existing countries are pressing for increased self-determination and autonomy. Some are going so far as to demand recognition as self-governing nations and are actively pursuing courses of political self-determination. Within the last two decades of the twentieth century Indigenous political movements have begun to redefine the relationships between colonizers and colonized peoples. In recent years Indigenous Peoples have managed to organize effectively in many areas of the world and have now brought their concerns to the fore, to be included in the political agendas of the nations they inhabit, and to be heard at the international level. If the levels of political self-determination that these Indigenous "nations" seek to achieve are realized in the future, their acquisition will alter considerably the present relationships of power worldwide, and lead to a redefinition of global geopolitical realities.

CHAPTER 2

PAST

COMMON THREATS OF THE PAST

Peoples on the land come and go. In the ebb and flow of a long and varied human history entire civilizations have been born, flourished, and died, many leaving but the merest traces of their existence. Cultures that imbue in their citizens an ethic of permanence are inevitably but flashes of momentary adaptation to environment when viewed from the perspective of man's time on earth.

Establishing a concept of "Indigenousness" to a particular landscape is difficult indeed, for not only do cultures and civilizations develop, mature, and pass into ruin, they also adapt, migrate, conquer and are conquered, or are subsumed or assimilated by others. While cultures evolve to perfect a form of adaptation to particular circumstances and environment, these too can change inexorably over time. Constant and unremitting change is itself the one constant of time.

Most, if not all, Indigenous Peoples are—within this framework—but the ultimate or penultimate manifestations of adaptation, merely the latest or next-to-latest actors to walk the stage upon which the resources that sustain life are laid. In Asia, where the majority of the world's Indigenous Peoples live, the tangled web of the history of previous human habitation is particularly difficult to decipher. In this cradle of humanity, entire civilizations have flourished and floundered over millennia on the same pieces of earth, leaving but scant traces in many overlapping layers underfoot. In many parts of Asia, today's habitations are built on cities built on cities built on towns built on camps, making moot many claims to previous occupation. In other continents as well, it can be shown that the present inhabitants are but the latest of a series of adaptations to environment and circumstance. There were previous inhabitants; there will be inhabitants in the future. Man's inherent ability to adapt will ensure people continue to populate the planet. While the nature of this inhabitation is changing and uncertain, its continuance is a certainty.

Yet, from the perspective of the present, the predominant form of economic adaptation, that of the modern industrial world economy, can

9

be seen to differ from previous economic adaptations in one crucial way: it is the first economy that is truly global in perspective. Previous economies have been based upon ecosystems. Modern citizens of the world have created something entirely new—an economy based upon the ecosphere that has erased all bounds of time and space.

In the past, peoples developed in isolation, surrounded by buffer zones that prevented the intrusion of unwanted influences. This is no longer the case anywhere in the world. The intrusion of the global industrial economy is the first truly unifying facet of man's material existence in history. The effects of modernity—be they good or bad, minimal or overwhelming—have now been felt by everyone everywhere. While the impacts and responses may be examined in considerable detail, the ultimate resolutions of global restructuring have yet to be determined.

From the Indigenous perspective, there is one simple aspect of capitalist industrial society that is totally overwhelming: its propensity for continuous expansion in search of the scarce resources of the planet. Abstracted to preindustrial terms, the basic concept on which industrial society is based—the growth of capital through the compounding of interest—is a phenomenon that is virtually incomprehensible from an Indigenous perspective. When Indigenous People stored five fish for future consumption, they expected there to be five fish in the cache upon returning. Modern society has invented a magical way of compounding savings. When industrial *Homo economicus* returns to the savings cache, he or she now fully expects there to be six fish where five were left.

Beginning in the fifteenth century, the peoples of Europe burst through the bounds that had kept human civilization up to that time essentially a localized phenomenon. Not only was the particular economic situation that prevailed in Europe at the time expanded to encompass great areas of the globe, but European peoples and philosophies and religions embarked on a period of expansionism unparalleled in the history of the world. In retrospect, it can be observed that a remarkable series of conjunctions coalesced in one time at one place. By the fifteenth century, the preconditions of the economic system that was to dominate the world were already in existence in its home continent.

European man, once deathly afraid of the evils that lurked in the forests at the edges of the realm, had done battle with the monsters that lived therein, and had won. To achieve the preconditions of his later industrial might, Western man had first to look within for a philosophical ethic that allowed for man's will to overcome nature. This he found ready at hand in a pervasive religion that decrees man to be master of all he surveys, to

10

be unquestionably God's chosen creation, dominant over all the earth, and over all others. Perceptually, the Christian religion fit European man to embark on the economic subjugation of the world.

For centuries, while the Indigenous Peoples of the planet were adapting to roles within the natural order, Europeans were busy creating a supranatural society largely freed of the constraints that nature imposed. By freeing themselves of bonds that tied them to their immediate environment, and by dominating that environment as no other society has ever done, Europe saw the gradual evolution of the primary condition necessary for the development of an industrial economy and an ethic that was to revolutionize the world: profit.

Christian Scripture explicitly condemns usury, as does Islam. For millennia, the collection of interest on loans was considered a sin within Aryan perceptions of morality, and was a process relegated to non-Christians. Yet, by the fifteenth century, this taboo was beginning to fall, as financial institutions began to emerge in response to identified needs for instantly obtainable capital for national enterprises and for mercenaries' wages. Christianity, at this juncture, was prepared to allow as much scope for profits as for prophets.

By this time the emergent nation-states in Europe had very nearly depleted their own sources of metal from which to make currency. Without ample supplies of coin with real and commonly accepted value there could be no real expansion of trade, and no further accumulation of transportable wealth. Bullion was not merely wealth in and of itself—it was also recognized as the means of obtaining wealth. Europe in the fifteenth century was desperately in need of gold, silver, and other measures of portable wealth to continue the economic experiment it had begun.

Social conditions, as well, were right for expansion. All areas of Europe had been repopulated with a vengeance after the ravages of the Black Death in the fourteenth century. After several generations of passing ever-smaller parcels of subdivided land from father to son to son, peasant landholdings had reached their ultimate capacity. There was no land left for second or third sons: their futures now lay outside the traditional primary pursuit of agriculture.

Warfare occupied a great many of them. By 1492, when the armies of Christian Spain had ousted the Moslem presence from Europe, Christopher Columbus had set sail for the New World. When he returned, there was a surplus of demobilized young Spaniards trained as soldiers, who had known no other profession and who saw few prospects of gainful employment elsewhere. As stories circulated in Spain of a New World filled with riches ripe for the taking, there was no shortage of eager, trained, and battle-hardened soldiers willing to enlist as maritime mercenaries.

Today, when we acknowledge the passing of five hundred years since the initial voyages of European discovery, it is important to remember that the world we now view from the western perspective was not opened by one man, but by countless Columbusses. The Renaissance voyages of discovery rank among history's two or three most important phenomena in terms of their ultimate effects upon the modern world. The Age of Discovery was not an anomaly but the culmination of a series of events that happened to coalesce in fifteenth-century Europe.

"Suddenly, there [was] an incredible outburst of daring, initiative, invention, constructive activity, not in one field alone, but in many fields at once" (Schumacher, 1976, p. 70). Europeans burst through the perceptual, philosophical, and geographical bounds that had restricted their sphere of influence for generations, and in the space of a few short years of expansion, forever changed the course of history.

By this time several key inventions had gained widespread acceptance in Europe: the compass, the cannon, gunpowder, armor, and a host of advances in shipbuilding, among others. Their wide-scale adoption had effectively propelled European man to a state of unparalleled technological superiority. Not only were these inventions useful, but their use was enhanced by a series of fortuitous discoveries. These included such mental constructs as a knowledge of how to sail a ship into the wind, how to effectively utilize the global patterns of wind circulation, and how to accurately record information on charts and maps. Seamanship, cartography, and navigation techniques improved considerably at this time, aided and abetted by the organized efforts of nation-states who found themselves to have a stake in the enterprises of nascent capitalist exploitation.

This concerted participation by governments in enterprises of exploration and discovery was, in and of itself, something entirely new. Where Spain led, and became fabulously wealthy in the process, Portugal soon followed. Not to be outdone, Holland, England, and France soon followed suit. In the race for riches that ensued, the competition to claim the world led to incredible efforts in which no major European nation could afford to lag.

With national pride at stake, the nations of Europe sought out hitherto unknown lands and carved up the world among them. For several centuries European explorers probed and charted new and unfamiliar waters and lands all over the globe, pausing just long enough to snatch a few natives as hostages, inquire as to the availability of local riches and resources, draw a map or two, and then return posthaste to the mother country to report upon their discoveries. In almost all instances the early European explorers were recognized immediately or in very short order by the Indigenous inhabitants of the worlds that they encountered for what they were: brutish, well-armed, technologically superior bandits intent primarily upon short-term prospects of pillage, plunder, and rape.

In nearly all of the new worlds they encountered, Europeans were able to establish an immediate ethic of dominance. In many cases there was no resistance offered, as the Indigenous Peoples clearly recognized the futility of opposition. The European invaders used the weaknesses of Indigenous Peoples against themselves, promoting civil wars, utilizing deception, cunning, fraud, and whatever subterfuge appeared necessary to accomplish the ends that were ultimately desired.

Especially in the early years of contact, the European conquerors made alliances among the stronger and better organized Indigenous Peoples when it was clearly to their advantage to do so. When the Spaniard Hernando Cortes landed in Veracruz in 1519 he encountered the Tlaxcala Nation, who had only recently come under the military domination of the Aztec Empire, and who had simmering resentments against their new masters. After conquering the Tlaxcala and others of similar ilk, Cortes enrolled them as allies against the Aztec, beginning a wave of such defections by former vassals of this empire, and ultimately spawning the seeds of its defeat. This ploy was also used in the subjugation of the Inca, the Maya, and in subsequent years was applied by both English and French in the eastern half of the North American mainland. Wherever the enemies of one's enemy could be conscripted as allies, they were. Europeans, it seems, have through long experience become masters of the strategy known as "divide and conquer."

Other times, the Europeans simply exterminated any groups of Indigenous inhabitants who happened to stand in their way. The word "haiti," an Indigenous term for mountains, survives as the name of a nation-state today. The Indigenous People who provided this word do not. They were exterminated by the Spanish within fifty years of first contact.

Following on the heels of the initial explorers—who not only showed the way to the new worlds they had discovered, but also pioneered the return routes back from the mother lodes of plunder to the mother lands—came the prophets of both commercial greed and religious proselytization. Coastal trading stations popped up all over the world from which missionaries, merchants, and more explorers probed and established commercial communication routes, expanding empires as alien bacteria destroy a living host, inexorably ever outward.

Tropical and subtropical plantations were established to fuel the Europeans' ever-increasing demands for raw materials and consumer goods. The plantations grew, thanks to the enterprise of individuals, a healthy profit incentive, and the labor of countless slaves. Eventually farming settlements were established by European economic émigrés intent on replicating the life that they knew in the Old World in the less crowded conditions of the New. Interspersed throughout were intermittent "rushes," as Europeans en masse sought either to capitalize upon a particular situation in the New World, or to escape a particular devastation in the Old.

The sum of five hundred years of European expansionism and hegemony has been the transcontinental movement of 100 million people away from their Old World homelands, and onto lands that were, for the most part, once used by the Indigenous Peoples of the world. As the European population bases have expanded, Indigenous Peoples have been increasingly marginalized in their homelands. As capitalism, industrialization, and modern technological revolutions followed the outward expansionism of Europe, their impacts have been disproportionately felt by the Indigenous Peoples of the world.

Faced with a common threat to their very existence, the many disparate Indigenous Peoples of the world are finding they share certain reactions. In a twist of historic irony, that which has served to destroy Indigenous cultures in the past serves as a basis for comparison in the present, and Indigenous Peoples the world over are now finding they have much in common.

THE IMPACTS OF THE PAST

Economies and cultures are intrinsically allied, and during human occupation of the planet many varied combinations of economies and cultures have existed. For an economy to develop, two primary conditions are required. First, there must be a sufficient supply of the resources needed to sustain human life over time. If a niche exists within the natural order, it will be exploited.

Second, to effectively establish an economy capable of utilizing the resources the environment offers, a critical human quality, ingenuity, must be taken into consideration. Provided with resources in sufficient quantity, all humans exhibit societal responses directed to the environment in an effort to sustain life. Given resources, and sufficient time to develop appropriate responses to environment, cultures develop.

The conjunction of resources and cultures, when attuned to human needs, produces a lifeworld. All lifeworlds, however, soon perceive their inherent limitations. All lifeworlds are fragile balances of competing variables, of dichotomies that must be rationalized with appropriate societal responses in order to continue to exist.

In the past, all societies have been forced to recognize that there are certain inherent limitations imposed by the very environment that sustains them. All societies have been acutely aware that their infinite capacity to expand eventually has to be balanced with a finite supply of resources. Human societies inevitably expand to fill their environmental niches to capacity, to probe the margins of the envelope of sustainability to the fullest, and to press at or beyond the borders of any limitations that may be imposed. The rationalization of population with resources produces, for any society over time, a sustainable carrying capacity characterized by an internalized knowledge of the exact limitations that the environment imposes. These balances are delicate—any changes over time or space can have severe consequences to any lifeworld, and to the people who live within it.

Disruptions in economic circumstance can be traumatic and inevitably lead to readjustments that test the mettle of a culture's powers of adaptation. Changes are inevitable, and all cultures have had to face the challenges that altered circumstances produce. Sometimes the resource side of the equation fluctuates; however, it is more often the case that the human side of the equation is disrupted, as one group of people seeks a proportionally greater share of scarce resources at the expense of another.

Conflicts created by expanding populations have characterized our entire existence on this planet. In the cutthroat world of economic competition, many models and modes of organization have emerged. All have been suited in some way to their environment, yet all have been repeatedly tested and challenged. If areal extent of economic control is used as a criterion of success, many empires can claim to have dominated territory in the past. Yet no system of economic control has ever achieved virtual domination of the entire planet, save one.

The present form of the emergent world capitalist economy has achieved a hegemony unprecedented in human history. Through a series of chance occurrences and favorable situations, we have created an economic reality capable of spontaneous regeneration, of expansion through time and space, that has grown unchecked to accommodate, for the very first time, a worldwide sphere of potential economic control.

While Europeans and their successor regimes have had the opportunity to accommodate themselves philosophically to capitalism over time, and have developed sophisticated mental mechanisms to utilize its positive strictures to their relative advantages, there are many peoples to whom accommodation has not come easily. Suddenly faced with an expansionist regime fed upon its own massive inertia, many of the Indigenous Peoples of the world have not been prepared for its ravages, nor have they escaped the disastrous consequences and crises that contact with this system has entailed.

No Indigenous societies could have possibly envisioned the scale of the forces allied against them at the time of first contact. In many cases immediate struggle was shown by demonstration to be futile, and in most cases the values of accommodation were proven to be as expedient as conflict in the face of overwhelming odds. In nearly all instances the dominant society came, saw, conquered, controlled, and simply annihilated all opposition.

DISEASE

In many instances death by disease, in massive numbers, decimated Indigenous Peoples at, or even before, first contact. Isolated by centuries of evolutionary development and distance, conqueror and conquered had developed differing immunities. Europeans had evolved, through countless deaths over many millennia, a certain amount of immunity to a select suite of diseases and a multitude of plagues for which the Indigenous Peoples of other continents had not. During the sixteenth and seventeenth centuries a series of epidemics of smallpox, chickenpox, measles, influenza, pneumonia, scarlet fever, yellow fever, and typhus swept through the Indigenous populations of the new worlds.

Wherever Europeans advanced, disease was sure to follow. Smallpox is thought to have arrived in the West Indies in 1518 (Berger, 1991, p. 27). There is no reliable estimate of the numbers of Indigenous Carib Indians alive in the West Indies at the time of contact, yet within fifty years they had been virtually exterminated on all major islands by smallpox and subsequent epidemics. Today Carib Indians can be counted in the dozens, virtually all of them of mixed blood and living primarily on one small Caribbean island: Dominica.

It has been estimated that, at the time of contact, the Indigenous population of the Americas was between 80 and 100 million. By 1550, approximately fifty years after the introduction of various European diseases, only 10 million remained (Berger, 1991, p. 29). In California the Native population fell from 120,000 to 20,000 in one thirty-year period, 1850–1880 (Burger, 1987). Even by a conservative estimate, at least eight out of every ten Indigenous Americans died of introduced disease in the sixteenth century alone.

Estimates of the populations of present-day Mexico at the time of contact range from a low of 12.5 million to a high of 25 million. By 1600, however, virtually all estimates put the remaining population at a high of no more than 750,000 (Bethell, 1984; Gibson, 1964). This represents a loss of Indigenous population in Mexico, in less than one hundred years, of at least 90 percent. Estimates for Peru, Ecuador, and virtually all the remaining areas of Central and South America are of similar magnitude for the years immediately following contact.

In other areas of the world the introduction of diseases ravaged Indigenous populations as well. In Australia the Aboriginal population, estimated at 300,000 before contact, had dropped to no more than 60,000 within one hundred years (Burger, 1990). In Tasmania the Indigenous population virtually disappeared within the same period. This decimation by disease at the time of initial contact continued unchecked throughout the history of contact and continues in many areas of the world today.

Between 1900 and 1957 the Indian population of Brazil dropped from over 1 million, by conservative estimates, to fewer than 200,000. In the fall of 1991 the last five Yaqui Indians of Bolivia were enticed out of their isolated forest environment. They know of no others who still live in the traditional manner in their jungle homelands. They now live in a pro-tected community far from their traditional territory with the remaining 130 members of their lineage (Tolan & Postero, 1992). Smallpox, cholera, and typhoid are rampant in the camp now. Few are expected to survive.

In many cases, the Indigenous populations were severely ravaged by the time Europeans arrived, the rapid spread of disease having preceded them. Pizarro subjugated the entire Inca Empire of 7 million people with an army of fewer than five hundred men, while Cortes conquered the Aztec Empire of 25 million with a band of just over five hundred mercenaries. In these cases, and in many others, disease was one of the conquerors' secret weapons.

The advent of epidemics is only one aspect of the great demoralization of Indigenous Peoples worldwide. Disease decimated Indigenous socie-ties to the point where many could no longer function as coherent entities.

With the leaders gone, with the food-gathering practices disrupted, and with the natural economies in chaos, many who had escaped the initial epidemics suffered from starvation and a loss of precious cultural knowledge of how to procure a livelihood. Demographic trends were altered and birth rates declined for generations (Berger, 1991, p. 30). Many formerly thriving Indigenous societies all over the world essentially collapsed in the face of overwhelming depopulation, never again to regain their vitality. Massive depopulation of Indigenous Peoples at the time of contact was a disaster on a scale virtually unparalleled in human history.

Of far more impact than population loss alone, however, was the cruel blow to the perceptual universes of Indigenous societies. Populations can be reestablished over time. Conceptual frameworks, whereby a people understand the very basic nature of their perceptual universe, cannot be reconstructed. Inferred inferiority can be insidious. Indigenous Peoples saw themselves failing in the face of diseases which they did not comprehend and for which they had no cures, yet the European invaders remained hale, hearty, and seemingly healthy.

The Indigenous reaction to this viral and microbial invasion called upon the supernatural, as traditionally ingrained and age-old prophecies of disaster were recalled and retold. This certainly reduced, in many cases, the Indigenous will to resist. Many Indigenous Peoples questioned the inability of their religious beliefs to adequately explain the new world they now faced. Traditional medicines had no effect on the new diseases, and old explanations of cause and effect no longer sufficed.

Faced with a world in which randomness existed beyond explanation, many Indigenous Peoples became profoundly disoriented and demoralized, and began to question and eventually abandon the beliefs that had once united their perceptual worlds into holistic and fully functioning lifeworlds. This sounded the death-knell for traditional religions. Without a complete parcel of metaphysical baggage, many Indigenous societies set out on the road to perceptual and psychological collapse in a new and radically altered world that no longer made sense, and in which cause and effect now assumed no culturally logical order whatsoever.

WARFARE

Indigenous Peoples soon discovered that death took many forms. In the end it was not so much epidemiological but technological superiority, especially of arms, that allowed the expatriate representatives of the Old

World to enforce economic control over the lands and resources of the New.

Warfare is a tool that allows one group of people to enforce their will upon another. Throughout human history, warfare has been a peripatetic fact of life, as one group of people seeks to dominate the lands and resources of another. Man is an organized and competitive animal, and nowhere is this more evident than in the ultimate finality of economic competition, the arts of war. History has shown us that peace is an aberration. If one society can expand by force, it will.

In most conflicts between peoples over resources and land, the group that possesses the superior technological capability, and the organizational capacity to ensure its continual means of production, tends eventually to predominate.

At the time when their rapidly expanding economic horizons began to come into contact with Indigenous Peoples throughout the world, Europeans did possess technological advantages, especially in the arts of warfare. These usually induced among the possessors of such technology an overriding ethic of brashness, boldness, and bravado, as they knew full well that they could call upon overwhelming force if needed in any dealings with the Indigenous Peoples they encountered. Every European at the edge of every frontier knew, or believed, that he or she had the armed might of empire and the divine right of purpose solidly behind every effort or action. For much of the period of contact, any concerted opposition on the part of Indigenous Peoples was interpreted as an occasion to call down the wrath of the full and focussed force of European military might.

Superiority of arms was used worldwide to subjugate to European will peoples who happened to occupy territory of value to the Eurocentric economy. Throughout the period of colonial expansion, Europeans consistently called upon their capacity and capability to kill, and occasionally to overkill, to demonstrate to any peoples that they happened to encounter the ultimate finality of the human equation, as expressed in their terms. In the end, and when all else is said and done, might was right.

Sharp steel and stinging lead inevitably followed any Indigenous challenges to the overriding economic will of the European expansionist enterprise. Although anger, resentment, and frustration could be focussed easily into hatred for the invaders, the overwhelming military superiority they possessed was, in most cases, immediately recognized, and with it the ultimate futility of armed resistance. An individual battle or two might be won, but, in the end, any war would inevitably be lost. To deliberately resist individually was an invitation to suicide, to do so as a people meant genocide.

On occasion armed resistance slowed the pace of colonial encroachment. The Aracanian Indians of southern Chile and Argentina successfully held off the Spanish and postindependence republics until the middle of the nineteenth century. In other areas alliances, diplomacy, and adaptation to the European technology of war were used to retain a sovereignty of sorts well into the postcontact period. The Indian Wars of the American West, which culminated in the defeat of General Custer at the Battle of the Little Big Horn in 1876, slowed settlement of the agricultural plains for a time. In vast and disparate areas of the world Indigenous guerrilla campaigns kept large numbers of colonial troops occupied for many years, and instilled fear in settlers. Yet settlement proceeded and the capitalist economy expanded incrementally to encompass the globe. In nearly all areas of this expansion, the relentless pursuit of territory and resources was aided, abetted, accomplished, and eventually consolidated by the threat, use, or abuse of armed force or warfare.

No society has perfected the arts of warfare and mass destruction in so complete a way as western industrial man. With this capacity and this capability, it was perhaps inevitable that western man and his military-economic system should some day come to control the world.

Warfare is now dominated by an awesome technology of destruction. Those who control this technology can enforce their dominion over others less advanced in the arts of annihilation. In many cases these struggles have been internecine, as various alliances of slightly differing Eurocentric and capitalist philosophical bent have battled to hold sway over parcels of territory viewed as vital to their continuing economic interests.

At the margins of these struggles, small bands of Indigenous Peoples looked on with detached indifference, as the industrialized peoples of the world proceeded to slaughter each other with remarkable efficiency. These are not their struggles. They take very little part in them. In the totality of Indigenous experience, they knew that these are merely competitions for dominance among people who manipulate an economic system that already has a firm control over their lives, their resources, their territory. From the Indigenous perception, from the perspective of the fragmented remnants of a precapitalist world, these disparate peoples know with certainty what the western mentality is only now beginning to discern: the first truly global conquest was not military but economic. The war was waged and won, one small battle at a time, against the Indigenous Peoples of the world.

Loss of Land

The Indigenous survivors of disease and open warfare soon learned that the colonialist interlopers had a far different concept of man's relationship to the land than they had. The Indigenous Peoples assumed that the land from which they secured a livelihood existed for their benefit. It was a communally held resource, if such a concept existed at all. For Indigenous Peoples, the land simply was, it existed, and free access and usage were simply unquestioned factors of existence. One could no more own the land, or parts thereof, than one could own the sky or the water. Without the landbase that sustained them physically and metaphysically, Indigenous Peoples have been cast adrift from the basis of their identity.

> Next to shooting Indigenous Peoples, the surest way to kill us is to separate us from our part of the Earth. Once separated, we will either perish in body or our minds and spirits will be altered so that we end up mimicking foreign ways, adopt foreign languages, accept foreign thoughts and build a foreign prison around our Indigenous spirits, a prison that suffocates rather than nourishes as our traditional territories of the Earth do. Over time, we lose our identity and eventually die or are crippled as we are stuffed under the name of "assimilation" into another society (Hayden Burgess, World Council of Indigenous Peoples, U.N. Testimony, Commission on Human Rights, 1985, from Burger, 1990, p. 122).

Indigenous Peoples were connected to the lands and resources around them in ways that western society still has difficulty comprehending. Most Indigenous societies drew their identity from the lands and resources around them, and had internalized themselves as people of the forests, of the plains, of the buffalo, or of the seal. They were products of the land, both physically and metaphysically, integral parts of the natural order, adapted through many generations of land use and occupancy to achieve a near-perfect compatibility within an environment they had come to internalize as their own.

The essential element of all Indigenous land use was a willingness to exist within the parameters of the natural environment as they knew and understood it. All Indigenous societies had perfected economic systems that were finely attuned to ecological balances, and that relied upon cooperative efforts to achieve sustainability within clearly identified biological niches. Many such niches existed, most were exploited, and widely divergent Indigenous societies grew to fruition within their confines.

When Europeans arrived, they carried with them a set of very different ethics concerning relationships to the land. Rather than live within the bounds of the natural order, Europeans maintained a profound belief that one could rise above these limitations to affect a mastery of human will over nature. Christians, it was assumed, had been created by God to triumph over the elements, and to impose their domination over the earth and all that is upon it.

Translated into terms that Indigenous Peoples all over the earth could readily comprehend, this meant quite simply that Europeans coveted the scarce lands and resources of the planet, and meant to acquire and own them for their own use, and for the benefit of their particular and peculiar economic system of organization. Simply put, Europeans were greedy. They had derived an economic model predicated upon greed, which, by its very nature, had to continually expand to exploit new areas and territories in search of the resources capable of sustaining it, or die. The momentum of this economic force eventually grew to surpass the bounds that had kept it contained on one continent. Hydralike, it began to reach out to others, and began the process of continuous expansion in search of resources and markets that continues to this day.

One of the fundamental concepts of this system is the right to individual ownership of lands, resources, and the means of production. Ownership confers certain inalienable rights, protected by the full force of law, including the right to exclusion. These rights can be bought, sold, traded, or inherited. Ownership is confirmed by a document known as a title. In order for a title to be recognized it must have some basis in law, and this requires the creation of a sophisticated system dedicated to the enforcement of this law. Much of the structure of legal systems of European origin relates to the evolved ethics of private ownership.

Although the strictures that relate to the legal aspects of property are common in most areas the world, this has not always been the case. All land was once unencumbered by individual ownership. At some point it had to become legally titled for the first time, to become a part of the system of property ownership now enshrined in law. In expanding from their traditional territories in the continent of Europe, Europeans have seen the enforcement of their particular concepts of private ownership in all other areas of the world. By what right, then, did Europeans and their successor regimes occupy, usurp, and first come to gain legal title to vast areas of land that were once the homelands of other peoples?

In answering this question we must bear in mind that this is an intellectual game in which the rules, indeed even the game itself, exist only within the parameters of the Eurocentric conception of legal reality. Private ownership of lands and resources was an alien concept to the Indigenous Peoples of the world before contact. Individual identities were subsumed by the collective will, as small bands of kin-and-clan were free to wander throughout territories in which they could create perceptual worlds of their own design, and in which human limitations were not enshrined in written law. In this fluid environment there were few borders. Those that did exist, existed primarily in the mind, and could be as easily conjured away as up. There were few firm fences, fewer walls, and no lawyers at all.

When Europeans began to discover that there were worlds beyond their own, at first their legal claims to these lands were based simply upon the "rights of first discovery." In some cases the mere sighting of a new land by an explorer entailed the establishment of such rights for the nation whose flag he flew. In other cases a captain and crew were put ashore to formally take possession of new territories in the name of the king or queen, and to raise the appropriate flag ashore. Often markings of such claims were placed in prominent places to advertise ownership.

Upon returning to the home port, the first duty of the captain of an exploration vessel was to report any discoveries that had been made to the proper authorities, who would duly record and eventually disseminate the new information. Once successfully accomplished, the essential value of any voyage of discovery was that it could be repeated. Once pioneered, trade routes developed to become the arteries of empire. Once established, they fed upon first discovery to sustain a claim against other European nations, and allowed for the creation of an infrastructure to fend off any competing interests.

Over the course of several centuries the entire world was "discovered" by European explorers from several nations, and, for the most part, parcelled out among them primarily on the basis of the rights of first discovery.

From the point of view of the peoples who happened to live in these newly discovered territories, however, there was nothing new. They knew where they lived. To be discovered by Europeans, to be included in their sailing charts, and to be accorded the privilege of having their homelands colored a particular color on maps made in Europe was somewhat beyond their ken and comprehension. From their perception, it meant very little at the time. From the perspective of historical hindsight, the audacity of one society to claim territorial supremacy over another merely by discovering where they live is oxymoronic in the extreme.

However, this was exactly how legal ownership evolved in many areas of the world, and prevailed during the early years of the European age of discovery.

At first, during the very early fifteenth-century expansion of Spanish interests into the Caribbean Islands, occupation was enforced by virtual extermination of the previous inhabitants. Indigenous Carib Indians, if they had not already succumbed to disease, were hunted down and slaughtered with horses and bloodhounds by the Spanish conquistadors for sport. The Spanish confirmed their title by eliminating the original titleholders.

Eventually, however, a certain amount of rationalization was necessary to reconcile the contradictions of claiming lands that were, in most cases, already occupied. For the Spanish, this formality meant the reciting of a simple verse, the "Requerimiento," which declared that Jesus was Lord of the Universe, that he had duly appointed St. Peter and his successors as Bishops of Rome, and that the Pope had bestowed the newly discovered lands of the world upon the Crown of Spain, and that this land was now being claimed in the name of the Crown. By virtue of the highest authorities of Heaven and Earth, this solemn declaration, proclaimed loudly in Spanish, was taken to be a legal claim upon the lands and resources, and even the people, that the Spanish had discovered.

Other European nations generally followed suit with some form of claim to discovered lands proclaimed in the name of the Crown. By merely declaring that a particular parcel of land was theirs, and by invoking a divine lineage of authority directly to God, the various great powers of Europe laid claim to much of the world. Their authority was, in many cases, enforceable in practice. By virtue of technological and military superiority, and by sheer audacity, many European nations enforced their claims to legal title over large areas of land. Large areas of frontier retain title as "crown lands" to this day.

On the mainland of North America, however, the Spanish encountered peoples of considerable sophistication, capable of offering effective and organized resistance on a scale heretofore unimagined. Clearly these were peoples who required military conquest to subjugate.

While it is true that the Spanish possessed a superiority of arms, that they were able to identify and effectively utilize internal dissensions in empires that they encountered, and were able to exploit the havoc wreaked by newly introduced diseases run rampant, the true secrets to their military conquests were centered solidly about the opposite extremities of the fundamental basis of military might: morale.

By the time the Spanish conquistadors arrived, Inca, Aztec, and Maya morale had sunk to perilously low levels after a series of blows that had served to disintegrate the connecting moral fabric of their existence. Decimated by disease, no longer able to call upon familiar connections between cause and effect, the moral and spiritual fibers that had held their societies together as functioning entities were in descendency at the very time when the conquering forces were in ascendency.

For the Spanish, therefore, bravado and brashness often sufficed where force of numbers failed. Morale enforced by steeled weapons and iron discipline ensured conquest over the demoralized societies encountered. For the first time, many Indigenous Peoples fought an enemy they could not kill. Their arrows merely bounced off the Spanish armor plate. Furthermore, the Spanish muskets could kill at a distance beyond which conflicts had traditionally been resolved. Horses added the strategic advantage of battlefield mobility, and terrified the Natives. Demoralization became endemic as the Indigenous will to resist collapsed in the face of new, innovative, and highly effective battlefield techniques. Even the Spanish were surprised by the ease with which they had acquired their vast new territories, and at their extent.

Once the conquest was complete, the Spanish faced the question of what to do with their new overseas possessions, and with the millions of people who lived in them. Philosophically, morally, and ethically Spain, and by virtue of proximity the rest of Europe, now had to rationalize on an intellectual basis the acquisition of overseas empires.

In 1550 the "enlightened" monarch of Spain, Charles V, summoned a collection of leading scholars of the day to the city of Vallodolid to debate the ethical question: "How can conquests, discoveries, and settlements (in my name) be made to accord with justice and reason?" This debate was to have far-reaching consequences for Indigenous Peoples the world over, with repercussions felt even today.

The protagonist for the status quo in this debate was Juan Gines de Sepulveda, Spain's leading philosopher of the day and foremost apologist. Following the then-prevalent views of Aristotle, who held the view that some races are inferior to others, Sepulveda argued that the innate superiority of European civilization based upon the one true religion, Christianity, justified and even compelled European man to subjugate all lesser peoples. The Indigenous Peoples, he stated:

> require, by their own nature and in their own interests, to be placed under the authority of civilized and virtuous princes or nations, so that they may learn, from the might, wisdom, and law of their conquerors, to practice better morals, worthier customs and a more civilized way of life (Hanke, 1974, in Berger, 1991, p. 21).

The Spanish, he argued, possessed the blessings of "prudence, genius, magnanimity, temperance, humanity, and religion," which the Indigenous Peoples did not. The "homunculi," literally little men not imbued with quite enough humanity to be called human, of the New World had no arts, letters, nor rule of written law or property. To these people, the Spanish brought gifts of immense value, such as iron, wheat, horses, sheep, goats, and pigs, as well as the immeasurable benefits bestowed by the arrival of advanced European civilization and Christianity. These gifts far outweighed the Spanish taking of gold, silver, lands, and liberties.

In simple terms, Sepulveda was arguing that European moral superiority alone allowed for absolute domination of the Indigenous Peoples of the world in the same way as it allowed for dominion over the natural world. This simplistic yet functional argument was to have a great impact on all Indigenous Peoples the world over.

The antagonist in this debate, an enlightened priest and sometime-citizen of the New World who had actually met Indian people, was Bartholome de Las Casas. He characterized the Indigenous Peoples he had encountered as rational human beings who had evolved civilizations and economies different from but nonetheless equal to those of Europe.

The entire system of colonial subjugation based on the edicts of the Requerimiento was flawed, he argued, as the Pope had no moral authority to exercise temporal authority over non-Christians. Conversion by force was morally unjustified, he argued, as Christ's message was to be spread by Christ-like and charitable methods. "Mankind is one," he proclaimed, and therefore all people should be treated with the basic respect that Scripture dictates. Indigenous Peoples were human, and had both souls and an inherent right to free will, he argued. The hitherto horrendous treatment of Indigenous Peoples in the New World at the hands of the conquistadors, and in the name of Christ and King, left no doubt in his mind that the lands had been acquired illegally.

According to Las Casas, from a Christian perspective, the only morally defensible position was the immediate return of all such wrongly confiscated lands to Indigenous Peoples, and with them the full rights to territorial sovereignty.

Another antagonist to the status quo of Spanish conquest at the time was the eminent political theorist and theologian Francisco de Vitoria. His teachings influenced a generation of scholars, who became known collectively as the School of Salamanica. Their influence can be seen as initiating early European attempts at establishing a form of international law, based upon the principles of law and logic.

Vitoria's lengthy but well-crafted arguments dismissed both the Papal Bull of 1493 and the basic principles of the Rights of Discovery as being extrajudicial, beyond the authority of the bodies of issue, and thus invalid in principle. Basing his views on interpretations of Aristotle, Vitoria went on to examine the argument of diminished responsibility then prevalent. Under this argument the Indians of America were viewed as being either slaves, or slavelike peoples subject to claim by the first masters to encounter them.

Aristotle had proclaimed that there were four categories of lesser beings subject to slavery: sinners, unbelievers, madmen, and totally insensate creatures. Members of the last two categories clearly did not possess sufficient comprehension to claim legal ownership of lands and resources in their own name, much less relinquish such rights. As for sinners and unbelievers, they too were subject to diminished responsibility, especially if enslaved.

As a slave cannot own anything of value, the lands that the Spanish had expropriated in the New World, Vitoria argued, were not the property of the Indians to give up in entirety. Furthermore, should the conditions of imposed slavery cease to exist in the New World, a certain amount of ownership would revert to the Indian Peoples, and reparations would be due, especially to those who converted to the Christian religion. Lands seized were thus held in trust, not fee simple title, and were to be encumbered with Indian claim until legally extinguished.

If, however, the Indians of the New World were not slaves but masters in their own lands, as Vitoria argued, then their lands should not have been alienated. Either way, he maintained, Sepulveda's status quo arguments collapsed in the face of reason. While the Spanish may have had a certain right to jurisdiction by right of conquest in America, Vitoria reasoned, these rights did not extend to the wholesale confiscation of all Indian lands and properties. By any legal or moral justification proffered, he concluded, Spain's claim to the unencumbered fee simple possession of lands in the New World was both spurious and refutable, and quite probably invalid.

These were radical arguments for the sixteenth century, as they are today. The debates at Vallodolid were followed with great interest by the Spanish monarchy. However, they never reached a formal conclusion, nor was any decision ever rendered. Although a Spanish Law of the Indies was promulgated to incorporate an accommodation with the Indian Peoples of the New World, it was never enforceable in practice. Events on the ground proved themselves capable of determining a status quo quite separate from the vagaries of philosophical and moral questions. In the end, the conquerors' dictum that "might makes right" was the ultimate arbitrator, as Spain and soon thereafter other European nations expanded from their heartlands to claim and place de facto title upon much of the newly discovered world as their own.

Apart from contractual arrangements between equals, there are essentially two ways in which ownership of anything of value can be wrested from a previous owner: theft and fraud. In a world in which there is an effective rule of law, both actions are illegal. In a world characterized by the absence of such rule of law, or the capacity to effectively enforce it, such actions become commonplace. Such anarchy exists at two levels: occasionally, in various times and in various places it has existed at a purely local level, and always it exists at a supranational level. On a stage where nations are players, there exists no global police force to enforce the rules of international justice. Nations have traditionally been allowed to take from others with impunity, and to enforce their will with might. Whether by outright theft, or couched in the seemingly subtler terms of fraud, control over much of the land and resources that were once Indigenous has now been alienated to the European mode of ownership.

To be fair, we must consider that outright theft as the alienation paradigm of choice waned somewhat with the introduction of other European nations into the race for world domination. As Spain reached the nadir of empire and began to consolidate its territories, England, France, Portugal, and later Holland began their ascendency as colonial masters in their own right. Beginning with the simple expedients of claiming sovereignty by right of discovery, these European nations evolved a series of subtle ruses to alienate new territories and to impose titles upon previously occupied lands.

However rationalized, the insidiousness of such tactics over time nevertheless had the same disastrous consequences for the previous occupants as had outright theft. Once owned, always owned: over time new and ingenious ways were discovered to wrest Indigenous ownership and impose legal titles to lands and resources.

One justification that was used was the expediency of underutilization. From the European perspective, any area of land without a permanent settlement and with untapped economic potential was deemed to be available for utilization. An agricultural people looked upon land far differently than did a hunting and gathering people. While most Indigenous Peoples tread rather lightly upon the land, leaving few signs of their passage, the arriving colonists began immediately to transform permanently by their labor the surface features of the new worlds in which they settled.

From a European common law perspective, the application of free labor and the effective control of freely available resources, if recognized and unchallenged, is referred to as first possession. If enforced, this possession is the root of title. To be enforced, an act of possession must be declared, communicated, and translated into the primary and secondary symbols that the culture understands. Clear markers of demarcation, both in physical reality and in text, advertise and enforce claims to ownership (Rose, 1985).

Nearly all early European settlements on Indigenous lands were marked with the permanent scars of both beacons of ownership and the products of human labor, and were in many cases fortified for defense. These markings signified, to the European legal establishment, the control of resources that ownership entailed. Once established, they tended to spread outwards; colonies begat subcolonies which, in turn, begat subcolonies until all available useful lands were occupied.

Often the simple act of continuous recognized occupation signified claim to ownership by Europeans. In many cases the exact areal extent of this occupation was challenged by other Europeans. Eventually the Crown would be called upon to consolidate and certify the status quo, most often within the cultural context of European common law, and ultimately to the advantage of the Crown. Peace, harmony, and the rule of law, it was found, led ultimately to prosperous settlers, who paid taxes and purchased consumer goods. After considerable experience, the Crowns of various European countries learned that there was both a profit to be made, and an advantage of avoiding litigation, by extending authority and title in advance of settlement. By the eighteenth century, control began to precede colonization.

In some cases the lands that Europeans aspired to control were truly vacant at the time of their arrival, as the diseases that had preceded them had depopulated huge areas. This was often viewed as a sign that conveyed divine authority on their enterprise.

In other cases there were survivors of the Indigenous populations to consider. At first, the notion of extinguishing previous title was an alien concept to colonial administrators, for how could people without any concept of ownership of the land lay claim to previous ownership? As the rationalist, liberal, and humanitarian concepts of European Enlightenment morality began to spread, the practice arose of agents of the Crown entering into agreements with various Indigenous Peoples to purchase the rights to occupy lands in advance of settlement. In most cases where these vague and ill-defined rights were purchased, they were paid for with baubles and trinkets of very little value. The true value of purchase was to assuage any guilt on the part of the new owners.

Eventually the various expansionary efforts of the European powers began to meet each other, and occasionally to overlap. These conflicting claims ultimately led either to conflicts in their own right, or became part and parcel of the frequent wars among European nations. National conflicts became colonial conflicts, and vice versa, as wars began to be waged on scales far wider than could have previously been imagined.

Many Indigenous groups watched these internecine conflicts with ambivalence, yet others saw that they could be turned to their advantage. By allying themselves with a victorious force, Indigenous groups with the prescience to pick a victor could secure advantages and powers for themselves. No Indigenous group mastered this technique more to their ultimate advantage than the Iroquois of Northeast America.

The Iroquois and their allies within the Six Nations Confederacy were a formidable force in their own right at the time of first contact with Europeans. The Europeans recognized their strength as the "keepers of the eastern door," the key to control over this part of the continent. They were actively recruited as allies by various forces, and collaborated at one time or another with many of them, ultimately to their own advantage. By forging astute alliances, they came to be viewed as the equivalent of a nation in their own right, and, as such, something of a new entity within the process of colonial domination.

As the Seven Years' War between the French and the English drew to a close, it became readily apparent that the English would win. Officially neutral during the better part of this war, the Iroquois Confederacy joined the British side in 1759. In 1763 they were rewarded by the victorious King George III of England with the formal issuance of a Royal Proclamation, a declaration that outlined certain principles of law that are still binding today. This Royal Proclamation of 1763 stated, in part, that, it being

> essential to our Interest, and to the Security of our Colonies, that the several Nations or Tribes of Indians with whom We are connected, and who live under our Protection, should not be molested or disturbed in the Possession of such Parts of Our Dominions and Territories as . . . are preserved for them, or any of them, as their Hunting Grounds, therefore any lands that had not been ceded to or purchased by Us as aforesaid, are reserved to the said Indians. Furthermore, We do hereby strictly forbid, on Pain of our Displeasure, all our loving Subjects from making any Purchases or Settlements whatever, or taking Possession of any of the Lands above reserved, without our especial leave and Licence for that Purpose first obtained.

The significant aspect of the Royal Proclamation of 1763 was its assertion that there was a necessity by law to extinguish Aboriginal title to the Crown before lands could be alienated, and that there was to be a legal extinguishment conducted by the expedient instrument of a contract: a formal and binding treaty between peoples of differing and competing interests. Over time, this precedent has secured a place within the process of the alienation of Indigenous lands, both within the English legal system and in consequent or subsequent derivations. This precedent has come to be known as extinguishment of claim by treaty.

In the United States this principle was upheld in a Supreme Court judgment of Justice John Marshall in the 1823 case of Johnson v. McIntosh (21 U.S. Wheat 543, from Berger, 1991, p. 75). Individuals, corporate entities, and states, it was ruled, could purchase Indian lands only from the Government of the United States, and then only after rightful treaty had been made extinguishing Aboriginal claim. This decision was refined somewhat by a later Marshall ruling in the 1832 case of Worcester v. Georgia (31 U.S., 6 Pet., 515, ibid., p. 76), to the effect that this process does not necessarily strip all rights but does leave Indian nations with certain legal interests in their ancestral lands and a certain degree of sovereignty intact.

However, this suggestion by the Supreme Court of the retention of certain undefined "diminished rights" was immediately rejected by President Jackson. Treaty or no treaty, Supreme Court judgment or not, President Jackson simply ordered that all Indians be moved, forcibly if necessary, west of the Mississippi River, as they had come to interfere with the orderly linear process of settlement and the progress of American civilization. Without Indians, no Indian title needed to be extinguished. Treaties, however, continued to be signed where Indians continued to live.

In time, and as legal title has come to be the standard by which ownership is measured, many treaties have been signed in the various areas of the world clearly occupied by Indigenous Peoples. Treaties are the legal basis by which many of the previously occupied Indigenous lands have come to be first titled and available for ownership. These treaties have taken different shapes and forms in various areas of the world. Although there are disputes as to their original intent and, in certain cases, their validity, the fact remains that many Indigenous Peoples the world over now live their lives within the legal confines and strictures of various treaties, and have surrendered a great deal accordingly.

The Royal Proclamation of 1763 also set a legal precedent by establishing the concept of "lands . . . reserved for Indians." While depriving preexisting peoples of lands and liberties, the process of treaty-making has also led, worldwide, to the establishment of certain defined lands where Indigenous Peoples may continue to live. Dispossessed of a majority of their traditional lands and resources, shunted onto marginal tracts far away from the mainstream of what has become an alien society to them, many Indigenous Peoples today face the prospects of either an assimilation into the dominant cultural milieu that surrounds them, or a profound estrangement and marginalization away from it.

MARGINALIZATION

In some nations of the world there are now specific areas set aside for Indigenous Peoples. They are known by many names: comarca, resguardos, adat lands, scheduled tribal lands, reducciones, or reservations. They are meant to be definable territories where Indigenous Peoples can continue to live a separate existence as remnants of a preindustrial economy, living museums of a preexisting order awash in a sea of change.

In other nations no provisions have been made to accommodate Indigenous Peoples. They are merely expected to fit into the changing economic order as best they can. Isolated, alienated, dispossessed of their lands and livelihoods, Indigenous Peoples all over the world have now come to share the same fate: a profound separation from the mainstream of societies that have taken them over, and then ignored them. Physically, perceptually, and culturally removed from the dominant societies that surround them, many Indigenous Peoples now exist in conditions of imposed internal exile, economic prisoners of a system beyond their comprehension, and in conditions that are beyond their control. The arrival of the industrial order has made many preindustrial Indigenous Peoples into marginalized peoples.

There is no question that Indigenous Peoples are at a great disadvantage in nearly all societies in which they live today. Economic discrimination is a fact of life faced by Indigenous Peoples worldwide. In Australia, 90 percent of Aborigines were reported relatively recently to be living below the national poverty line (*Asian Times,* Jan. 11, 1984, in Burger, 1987, p. 183). In the Northern Territory, where many of the Aboriginal Peoples of Australia live, twice as many of their people are reported in the very lowest income bracket as the population at large (Australian Bureau of Statistics, 1990). In Orissa State in India, 87 percent of bonded laborers, a system virtually akin to slavery, were found, a decade ago, to be from Indigenous Scheduled Tribes (U.N., 1982). This situation has not changed. It is estimated that upwards of 90 percent of the Amehusha and Yagua Indian tribes of South America are virtual slaves to the patron debt-bondage system that operates there. Landowners and employers in these areas monopolize the importation, distribution, and sale of necessary supplies, and by offering long-term credit at high rates of interest, they can enforce total economic hegemony. This system of lifelong and virtually inescapable debt of servant to master is also widespread in Peru and in the Amazon Basin of Brazil (Burger, 1987, p. 99).

In the United States, average per capita yearly income for Indians is the lowest of any identifiable segment of the population, lower than that of Blacks, and less than one-half that of Whites (Burger, 1987, p. 22). In Japan, Indigenous Ainu income remains significantly less than the Japanese average (de Vos & Wetherall, 1983, p. 13). In Canada, "Indians consistently earn about two-thirds that of non-Indians, regardless of the level of [similar] education" (Armstrong, 1990). Even in the comparative affluence of Scandinavia, Indigenous Sami have a standard of living measurably lower than their non-Sami neighbors (Burger, 1987, p. 180).

Indigenous Peoples, wherever they live, are more likely to be unemployed than are members of the dominant population. In most industrialized nations, Indigenous Peoples are the last to be hired, and the first to be fired. In many places they constitute a reserve labor force called up only if the situation warrants. Otherwise, they are left to eke out an existence as best they can. In the United States, Indigenous unemployment rates are four times higher than the average, in Canada and New Zealand five times, and in Australia more than six times (Burger, 1987, p. 22). In many areas of the world Indigenous Peoples are employed only seasonally, if they are employed at all. Income disparities, when compared with the status of the dominant societies in which they live, are a fact of life for nearly all Indigenous Peoples today.

In many areas of the world, Indigenous Peoples lack even the basic educational prerequisites necessary to function in an economic system that values literacy. Most Indigenous societies do not have the educational opportunities that would equip them to compete for employment. In India, only 11 percent of the Indigenous population is classified as literate, in Guatemala only 12 percent. In Indonesia, Brazil, Paraguay, Malaysia, and in many more countries, Indigenous education levels average less than two years of primary school. In the United States the average is five school years, with a drop-out rate for Indigenous students more than double the national average (Burger, 1987). In Canada, fewer than one-quarter of Indigenous students finish secondary school (Armstrong, 1990). Even when they do manage to acquire a modicum of education, many Indigenous People face discrimination in a workplace that rewards its own to the exclusion of all others.

Indigenous Peoples are liable to be marginalized medically as well. In many areas of the world lower standards of living are translated into far higher rates of mortality for Indigenous than for non-Indigenous populations. In Australia the average Aboriginal lifespan is a full twenty years shorter than that of a White Australian (Australian Bureau of Statistics, 1990). In Brazil, Paraguay, and Guatemala Indigenous lifespans are a decade shorter than the general population's (Burger, 1987, p. 24). In the United States, as much as 95 percent of housing on Indian reserves has been described as "dilapidated, makeshift, unsanitary, and crowded" (ibid.). In Mexico, it is estimated that a full 97 percent of the Aboriginal population lacks basic sanitary services such as clean water or proper sewage disposal (ibid., p. 24).

34

These litanies of statistics can be repeated consistently throughout the Indigenous diaspora of the world today. Whatever area of investigation is pursued, the inescapable fact remains that Indigenous Peoples are at a considerable disadvantage. In this century alone at least eighty-seven Indian groups in just one country, Brazil, have become extinct (Ribiero, 1957). Faced with conquest, diseases, expulsion from their traditional lands and territories, and ever-increasing marginalization at the very fringes of a dominant and dominating larger society, it is a wonder that many Indigenous Peoples have survived these onslaughts of the past, and more, to exist at all into the present.

CHAPTER 3

PRESENT

THE REALITY OF THE PRESENT

Lifeworld is a whole, composed of the entire sum of its parts. Culture, economy, resources, technology, territory: all are intrinsically connected. For human societies, reality exists as perceived. It is, in its entirety, a phenomenon created in the human mind.

Every culture evolves to eventually create a mental matrix that allows its initiates to synthesize a collection of seemingly random sensate experiences into a coherent view of the whole. By utilizing these organizational connections, and by passing them on and adding to them over generations, a people can compile an accumulated knowledge of the world around them, and can interpret this world in a way that makes sense within the evolved framework. Intimate knowledge of any particular environment can allow for connections to be made between cause and effect, and can assure prediction with confidence. Through knowledge evolved through experience of place into culture, a human framework exists whereby perception of environment becomes a people's internalized lifeworld.

Yet the warp and woof of the fabric through which these myriad mental connections are tied together are exceedingly fragile. Each strand of every aspect of every culture is being continually tested against the exigencies of a harsh reality. For any culture to be complete, all aspects of reality must be woven into a coherent and self-sustaining entity, a complex pattern that is able to explain the world in its entirety to its initiates. When one aspect of this world changes inexplicably, when cause and effect are somehow no longer connected in a culturally logical sequence, and when predictions can no longer be made with certainty, the entire fabric is weakened. When many changes occur at the same time, their inherently interconnected effects can be compounded. Rapid and overwhelming change can tear at the threads that bind a culture together and make it a whole. The sudden intrusion of what seems like massive randomness into a society challenges its capacity for explanation, and can ultimately threaten its very existence.

For Indigenous Peoples today the intrusion of industrial time and space poses a very real threat to selected aspects of their traditional lifeworlds. All aspects are challenged by an overarching alien society intent upon domination. This society has an inherent belief that its ways are superior in all aspects. The dominant society has internalized an ethic of evolved superiority. In this ethic, any society that has not evolved in the same manner as it, that has not progressed through the same sequences and internalized the same core values, is deemed to be "primitive," and in need of change, whether it wants it or not.

This dominant society has now carved up the entire planet into realms of authority. Each dominant society has identified specific groups of Indigenous Peoples and has labeled these societies as "their" Indigenous Peoples. Each dominant society is, or at least once was, fully intent upon, in their own words, "making them more like us," of changing all aspects of the "primitive" societies who live among them to conform to the expectations the dominating society imposes.

In many areas of the world the dominant societies have erected bureaucratic entities specifically to directly administer all aspects of the lives of their Indigenous minorities. Monolithic institutions such as the Bureau of Indian Affairs in the United States, the Department of Indian Affairs and Northern Development (in its most recent reincarnation) in Canada, the Department of Aboriginal Affairs in Australia, and FUNAI (the National Indian Foundation) in Brazil have come to be pervasive influences in the daily lives of the Aboriginal citizens whose lives they direct. In most cases they have been remarkably adept at enforcing outward manifestations of behavioral change upon the Indigenous Peoples they administer.

This domination has had a profound effect upon all Indigenous Peoples of the world. Where once they lived in a lifeworld in which cause and effect were linked in culturally logical terms, the intrusion of an alien industrial ethic has caused massive disruptions, and has severely challenged their ability to know and to understand the new world in its entirety. Colonialism, masked as progress and modernity, and its attendant hegemony, has had a destructive effect on precolonial peoples.

Little by little, bit by bit, Indigenous Peoples have seen limits inexorably placed on the bounds of their existence, a slow yet uniformly linear series of restrictions imposed by the intrusion of a dominant society intent upon securing the scarce resources of the planet for industrial use, and of enforcing its will. The continued weakening of various threads from the cultural and economic matrix has seriously threatened the strength of the fabric of culture and economy from which their lifeworlds were once woven.

For Indigenous Peoples today, these threats are both economic and social. While economic colonialism—the alienation of lands and resources and the imposition of capitalism—threatens a people's way of life, it also has implications that resonate throughout the social fabric of the societies involved. Without a fully functioning economy, a way of securing a livelihood, a people's entire culture is in danger of collapse.

The economic threats to Indigenous Peoples today can be divided into two components: those that have taken place and those that are taking place. In many areas of the world the lands and resources that were formerly Indigenous have now been alienated from them. In many of these areas traditional economies are no longer viable.

In order to continue to exist, Indigenous Peoples have had to adapt to the perceived needs of the dominant cash economy, and to assimilate the demands of economic modernity. No longer able to secure a fully sustainable traditional and culturally understood livelihood on the small parcels of territory to which they have been exiled, many have chosen to make the move from their traditional homelands to the burgeoning city life, and to become semi-assimilated into the dominant urban culture. In both Canada and the United States, the majority of Indigenous People now live away from their reserves in urban environments. In New Zealand over three-quarters of the Indigenous Maori now live in cities.

There are areas of the world where Indigenous Peoples still retain a semblance of their traditional territories, resources, and economies, and where traditional Indigenous economies retain a modicum of viability. For the most part, these are at the very edges of accessibility, such as the far margins of tundra, jungle, or marginally productive ecosystems beyond transportation networks that have escaped the attention of commercial interest until now. Hunting, gathering, fishing, nomadic pastoralism, slash-and-burn agriculture, and other preindustrial pursuits are still practiced in some locations today, and provide a vital link to the lands and resources that have always tied Indigenous Peoples to place. Yet even in these areas there are threats to traditional Indigenous pursuits.

FRONTIER MIGRATIONS

Of these threats, perhaps the greatest has been and continues to be the large-scale migration of non-Indigenous People onto Indigenous lands. The world has probably never experienced as massive a movement of population as the transmigration of Europeans away from their home continent in the past several centuries. Not only have Europeans migrated in massive numbers, but their descendants have continued the inexorable expansion unchecked.

In the search for lands and resources to sustain this global economic expansion, it has generally been Indigenous Peoples who have been and continue to be displaced to make way for the new economic order. In simplistic terms, Indigenous systems of production are not intensive and require large areas of land in order to be sustainable. From the perspective of agricultural and industrialized societies this amounts to an underutilization of lands and resources. As human populations expand, and as presently exploited resources continue to be depleted, expansion at the frontiers is inevitable. Yet in most cases, there are Indigenous Peoples living in these frontier areas. Inevitably, some accommodation with these peoples must occur as the margins of modern industrialized civilization expand ever outward.

Transmigration is one way of utilizing frontier areas. Faced with overpopulation in one area, and relative underpopulation in another, many governments have chosen the simple and expedient solution of relocation. Today, there are officially sponsored or implicitly sanctioned large-scale resettlement programs underway in Brazil, Peru, the Philippines, China, Bangladesh, and Indonesia.

Perhaps nowhere is this process more pervasive than in Indonesia. In this island republic, with the fifth largest total population in the world, over 60 percent of the people live on 7 percent of the land. The island of Java is, today, the most densely populated place on earth. There is great pressure imposed on the central government to find room for expansion to ease the situation in Java and on the other severely crowded islands of Madura and Bali. Financed partly by the World Bank and various foreign aid allowances, Indonesia embarked on an ambitious program of relocation in 1969. This policy is called "Wawasari Nusantara," which can be translated as "The Indonesian Archipelagic Outlook." By the end of the present plan in 1994, more than 10 million people will have been resettled to other islands (Burger, 1990). In most cases, this relocation has been at the expense of the Indigenous Peoples of the outer islands, who do not welcome this massive intrusion onto their traditional lands.

Conquest by numbers has been the fate of many of the Indigenous Peoples of the world. In an age in which democracy has emerged as the paradigm of choice for many governments, the concept of the greatest good for the greatest number has tended to overwhelm the ability of Indigenous minorities to influence events in their traditional territories.

The interests of small populations tend to give way to larger populations in a democracy. Faced with the reality of demography, the 4 percent of the world's population that is Indigenous will have a difficult time averting subjugation by the tyranny of numerical superiority, as the dominant societies continue to flood into their traditional territories.

Resource Extraction

There are other serious threats posed by the dominant societies. In the competition for resources, traditional Indigenous sustainability has been profoundly affected by the dominant ethic of immediate and large-scale exploitation. Forestry, agribusiness, mining, the damming of rivers, and other industrial activities have had a great effect upon Indigenous Peoples.

Approximately 50 million of the world's Indigenous People today live in the world's rainforests (Burger, 1990). These rainforests contain many resources that can be effectively exploited for profit by industrial societies. Although many Indigenous People continue to rely upon the forests as a basis for their traditional economies, the forests are disappearing at an alarming rate.

At the present rate of exploitation, by the year 2000 there will be virtually no primary forests left in Guatemala, India, the Philippines, Malaysia, and Thailand. In these countries alone between 7 and 8 million Indigenous People will lose their traditional livelihoods (Burger, 1990, p. 88). In Brazil, it is estimated that over half of the remaining rainforest will disappear by the turn of the millennium, and only small remnants will be left in most other areas of the world (ibid.). Yet there is continued pressure to continue cutting.

Much of the remaining rainforest is viewed as potential income sought and sorely needed by developing nations in their march to maturity within the dominant world economic order. World demand for wood remains high. In Japan alone, tropical hardwood imports have increased over twenty times since 1950. As the forests decrease, prices will increase until the resource base is depleted, and with it the livelihoods of the Indigenous Peoples who inhabit the forests.

Damming of rivers for hydropower to fuel the industrial economy has also had a great effect upon Indigenous economies in recent decades. Many of the world's great rivers are of fundamental importance to the Indigenous inhabitants who live along their margins. In many cases the river was called, within the Native language, simply "the river." In most cases this concept was untranslatable to outsiders, as the river and its resources were virtually inseparable from life itself and occupied a position at the very center of existence. Without the river many Native cultures would cease to exist, and most Indigenous Peoples had no concept or comprehension of a power that would ever be able to deny their rivers to them.

There are presently over one hundred superdams on the great rivers of the world. Forty-nine of them were built in the 1980s. Virtually all of them have been built on Indigenous lands, or lands claimed by Indigenous Peoples (Burger, 1990, p. 96). Many more are under construction, or are being planned. For an industrial and industrializing world with its massive basic need for energy, hydroelectricity appears to be the answer to a cheap, convenient, and expedient power source for the future. This demand will continue to have disruptive impacts on large areas of land. For Indigenous Peoples who presently live on this land the social and economic costs will be devastating.

In recent years over 100,000 Chakma tribespeople in Bangladesh, over 50,000 Tucurui, Itaipu, and other forest dwellers in Brazil, and over 3 million members of National Minorities in China have been forced from their traditional lands by damming. The massive Narmada Dam Project in India will displace at least 80,000 Bhil, Bhilalas, Vasaras, Tadaris, and Ratras in its first phase alone (Burger, 1990, p. 99). The second phase of the James Bay Project in northern Quebec will, if it proceeds, affect an area of land that is larger than many of the smaller nations of the world.

These dams have wider costs beyond displacement, many of which are felt by Indigenous Peoples alone. Siltation leads to loss of bottom fertility, which leads to increased organic decomposition. The hydrogen sulfites lead to increased levels of toxic materials such as mercury, which poisons the fish upon which many local Indigenous economies depend. Ecosystems are disrupted in ways we are only now beginning to understand, and for which we presently have no effective prescriptive solutions. There are unintended consequences still beyond our capacity to fully comprehend, yet the damming of rivers continues unchecked, and will inevitably continue to threaten the ways of life of the Indigenous Peoples who live on their margins.

Non-renewable resource extraction also threatens Indigenous Peoples in many areas of the world today. Mining and petroleum exploration tend to be concentrated in frontier areas. In Australia nearly all mineral reserves are on lands claimed by Aboriginal Peoples. In the United States 25 to 50 percent of all uranium, one third of the coal, and 2 percent of oil and gas reserves are located on Indian Reserves (Burger, 1990, p. 102).

In Canada a significant amount of mineral wealth yet to be tapped lies on lands claimed by Aboriginal Peoples. The largest undeveloped coalfield in the world lies in the heart of Guajiro Indian lands in Colombia. Asia's largest iron ore deposit, at Bailadilla in India, is in the center of lands claimed by the Indigenous Dandami. In Russia the vast majority of mineral production continues to take place on Indigenous lands, without the consent of those living there. The second most important source of nickel outside Russia is on Kanaky lands in New Caledonia. In Brazil, the encroachment of a ragtag army of *garimpieros,* small-scale gold miners, has created a Wild West gold rush that threatens the continued existence of the Indigenous Yanomami and other rainforest tribes in the very heart of their traditional territories.

Mining and non-renewable mineral extraction are probably the greatest threats to whatever remnants of Indigenous economies survive in the world today. These traditional economies retain a semblance of viability precisely because they have been situated at frontiers, a safe distance from the effects of large-scale industrial intrusion. The isolation that has somewhat protected the traditional Indigenous economies, and their cultural identities, is the reason these areas are poised to experience an enormous onslaught in coming years. As the dominant society has exhausted its own resources on its own territories, it is now seeking out and exploiting the resources to be found at the frontiers. This industrial resource expansion will continue to have devastating consequences on the Indigenous Peoples who live on the frontier margins.

MILITARY ACTIVITY

As the strategic military values of frontier lands have become increasingly evident, many Indigenous Peoples have been directly affected by the escalating processes of militarization. As time and space have been compressed by modern technological prowess, locations at territorial margins have assumed increasing strategic military value to many nations of the world. Borders have become precisely defined meeting points of territorial sovereignty. In many cases these borders are the exact intersections of competing economies, philosophies, and ideologies, with vast differences between often-conflicting regimes of human organization meeting at one artificially demarcated line on the earth.

All governments are prepared to resort to military force to protect the sanctity of their borders against all threats, actual or imagined. They are also fully prepared to use force to suppress any internal threats that might in any way hinder their military capacity within their defined borders. In the maintenance of military sovereignty in an era in which the possibilities of total war have been amply demonstrated, all aspects of a nation's life must ultimately be subservient to the overriding interests of national security, however perceived.

When faced with any issue in which national security is involved or invoked, the exercise of individual free will becomes immediately subservient to the will of the state. In the interests of national security all actions by the state can be rationalized without recourse to further reason. In all nations of the world national minorities are fully expected to immediately support the will of the majority if interests of territorial sovereignty or security are invoked. Often this expectation has led to simmering resentments, especially among those minorities whose own versions of national self-determination conflict with those of the dominant majority.

There are many instances in which Indigenous Peoples in frontier areas have now taken up arms in their efforts to assert their own national self-determination, or to protect themselves from the perceived threat of military domination by an alien entity intent on enforcing its own version of sovereign control. Since the end of the Second World War, over one hundred new nations have emerged from the largely artificial borders left in the wake of colonial empires. Many of these can trace their birth to the efforts of armed national independence movements. In many nations of the world today, Indigenous Peoples are asserting their own sovereignty by arms in an effort to secure a place as recognized members of the world club of independent nations.

At the moment there are active and armed Indigenous struggles for national independence in Myanmar (Burma), Laos, India, Bangladesh, Iraq, Iran, Turkey, Indonesia, Ethiopia, Sudan, Guatemala, Nicaragua, and the Philippines. If guerrilla activities are taken into consideration, this list could be expanded considerably. Of the approximately 120 armed conflicts in the world today, almost three-quarters can be identified as struggles between centralized state governments and peoples who identify themselves as distinct ethnic nations living within their borders (Burger, 1990, p. 108).

In some areas these struggles have met with some success. The Karen of Myanmar, allied with other Indigenous Peoples, have effectively established their own nation-state, Kawthoolei, in the "Golden Triangle" area, but have been unsuccessful in securing international recognition. In Africa, the Eritreans have only recently achieved full nationhood, after a quarter century of armed struggle. In other areas Indigenous Peoples have been less successful in challenging the armed might of existing nation-states, and have suffered greatly. There are now over 14 million political refugees in the world. Many of them are displaced and dispossessed Indigenous People.

Many nation-states have invoked the overriding concerns of national security to justify militarization of frontier territories occupied by Indigenous Peoples. Military activity is a common occurrence on Indigenous territories all over the world. The need for space in which to conduct war games and training exercises has turned many an Indigenous landscape into a military playground.

To date, perhaps the most insidious effects of peacetime militarization—justified by concerns of national security—upon Indigenous Peoples have been related to the development of atomic weaponry. Nearly all nuclear testing has been conducted on lands that are occupied or claimed by Indigenous Peoples. The United States has detonated over 650 atomic reactions on lands claimed by the Shoshone alone (Burger, 1990, p. 108). The former Soviet Union detonated an unknown number of nuclear weapons on territories occupied by Indigenous Peoples in Central Asia and Siberia. The Russian government has now revealed that every person born in Kazakhstan before the 1963 suppression of open-air atomic testing, approximately 40 percent of the present population, may suffer from some form of radiation-related sickness to some degree or other. Populations in other areas of the former Soviet Union may also be at risk, including Indigenous Peoples in the Russian far north. In China, the Uighur Tribal Minorities are now presenting claims that the large-scale testing of Chinese nuclear devices in their territories was conducted without their permission, and has left a significant number of their people affected by long-term health problems (Burger, 1990, pp. 108–110).

In the Pacific, home to over 6 million Indigenous People, the detonation of over two hundred atomic weapons has vaporized six formerly inhabited islands and rendered a further fourteen islands uninhabitable. Many islanders have had to be relocated, and there are now indications that there may be long-term health risks associated with nuclear testing in the area. France no longer releases any medical statistics relating to Indigenous Peoples in French Polynesia.

Few Indigenous Peoples anywhere in the world today remain unaffected by military activity. Militarization has taken, and continues to take, its toll. In the struggles for control of land and resources, as the modern military-industrial complexes compete for and consolidate their claims to various slices of the world, the preexisting peoples have found themselves caught up in conflicts that are not of their own creation, and that in many instances are beyond their comprehension or control. Many now have had primary experience with Kalashnikovs, AK-47s, M-1s, rocket launchers, and other assorted paraphernalia of modern warfare. Some have now internalized their form and function, and ultimate usefulness, into their perceptual parameters.

COMMON IMPACTS OF INTRUSION

The impacts of the entire suite of events that colonialism and continuous contact have created have forced all Indigenous Peoples of the world into a difficult situation, one in which they must now begin to assert themselves, and to initiate an active struggle to insure their continued survival. Whether military or industrial, resource extractive or agricultural, wave after wave of uninvited alien intrusions have affected all Indigenous societies. In most cases the sequence of events has been remarkably similar.

From the Indigenous perspective, all the alien intruders were essentially the same. Of whatever ilk, and clothed in whatever costume or symbol of authority, there was perceived to be a consistency of purpose. As wave upon wave of industrialized invaders overwhelmed their societies, and as they were kept reeling from one crisis to the next, never given time to fully recoup, their societies began to crumble around them. In the face of what appeared to be a concerted, deliberate, and long-term assault on the values they held dear, Indigenous Peoples faced a monumental tide of change. This tide appeared to change only its form, its outward manifestations, but not its function or effects over time. Bureaucrats followed settlers who followed traders who followed missionaries who followed explorers in unending sequence. All, it seemed, shared the same allied inner purpose: a profound alienation of Indigenous Peoples from all aspects of their former lives, accomplished one aspect at a time by competing agencies of unrelenting change.

Inevitably, preexisting peoples have found themselves inexorably tied to the alien economic order and dependent eventually upon certain aspects of it for their survival. Modernity has addictive qualities that preindustrial peoples have found difficult to resist. By carefully cultivating a desire for the material incentives it can offer, industrial society creates an inherent dependency on them and thus a market for its goods and services. Given rifles, there is a need for bullets. Once an outboard motor is obtained, there is a continuing need for parts and gasoline. Alcohol and tobacco create their own dependencies.

Once the delicate balance of any localized economy has been disturbed by outside influences, repercussions ripple throughout the system. In many areas of the world, the introduction of rifles, for example, has altered the fundamental relationships of Indigenous Peoples with their game supply. Often, formerly functioning facets of the preexisting economies have not been able to survive the intrusions fully intact.

Faced with the loss of land and livelihood, many Indigenous Peoples have found survival difficult in the postcontact period. Caught between two worlds, they do not fit easily into either. Separated from the traditions and beliefs of the past and not yet fully integrated into the realities of the present, many Indigenous People have struggled to find a meaningful identity in a changing world that their cultural constructs cannot fully and adequately define.

It is only in recent years that various groups of disparate Indigenous Peoples have come together to discuss their common circumstances. In doing so, they have discovered that they have had a remarkably similar series of reactions to the Eurocentric expansionism that has dominated the past several centuries of world history. While they were at home in their various territories, this tide of change engulfed them all in a unitary flow. The shrinking of time and space this has entailed has brought the world to their doorsteps. The buffers and barriers that once allowed for the separate evolution of all peoples are now being swept away as the world becomes a global commons.

For the buffered minorities of the past, the present reality of a global interchange of people, ideas, and commerce has meant a crisis of identity. The outside world, once distant, dimly understood, and exotic, is now part and parcel of daily existence. With its intrusion, an entirely new series of problems is posed, a set of choices very nearly beyond comprehension. The actions, whether intended or not, of the past and of the present are creating precedents that will inevitably persist into the future.

Within this accelerated merging of the peoples of the world, new identities have emerged at a previously unprecedented rate. The mixing of cultures and races has formed everywhere new combinations of peoples with complex ancestries. In some cases new and vital cultural identities, such as the Métis of Canada, have emerged. In many cases, however, the margins have now become blurred as bloodlines blend into a global superorganism. It is difficult to find a full-blooded Indigenous Hawaiian or Carib or Lenca or Vedda today. The connecting factors of once-strong bloodlines have been mitigated by centuries of cultural contact and genetic blending.

For Indigenous Peoples everywhere, this problem of identity poses grave concerns. In a dominant society characterized by linear precision and finite parameters, Indigenous Peoples unfamiliar with quantitative concepts are now being forced to define themselves in new and unfamiliar ways. In many cases it is the dominant societies in which they live that provide the parameters for the definitions of Indigenous Peoples, as they strive to label and identify the people they count as citizens.

In some cases this external labeling has resulted in a confusion of classification for Indigenous Peoples. Different labels have resulted often in differential treatment at the hands of the external agencies entrusted with fiduciary obligations towards their Indigenous wards. This differential treatment has, in many instances, merely served to exaggerate slight cultural differences among and between various groups of Indigenous Peoples who have found themselves so labeled. For the dominant societies, this tactic of "divide and conquer" has proven to be an effective way to prevent the evolution of Pan-Indigenous alliances, and to retain effective control over smaller and smaller definitional entities.

The litany of the symptoms of contact is remarkably similar among all Indigenous cultures on all inhabited continents. Loss of cultural identity inevitably leads to manifestations of individual frustration and escapism. Alcohol and drug abuse, petty crime, overrepresentation in prison populations, low levels of education and workforce participation, grinding poverty, high rates of suicide—all are aspects of life that serve to characterize many Indigenous realities of today.

The symptoms of cultural contact gone awry are present for all to see. What has taken the dominant society generations to effectively internalize within their cultures must be accelerated in the new round of time and space compressions that characterize Indigenous lifeworlds today. All Indigenous Peoples, wherever they live, are intimately familiar with this frenetic pace of change. For them, the dominant fact of life has become unrelenting change itself, as all aspects of life undergo a constant process of reinvention and reinterpretation.

Within this process a series of identity crises is inevitable, as constant redefinition leads to anomie. It is difficult to survive a crisis, more difficult to survive several, and exceedingly difficult to survive a seemingly unending series. Cast adrift, Indigenous Peoples are everywhere attempting to reposition their cultural anchors in a sea of change.

Within this world there is a great incentive to address the problems that face them one at a time. There is great danger inherent in this approach, however. By treating only the symptoms of the problems, and then in most cases only minimally, the root problems remain.

By discussing the common threads of the Indigenous experience of the world today, among themselves and in international fora, many such groups are now discovering a unification of purpose that goes beyond the individual symptoms of distress. By examining the common aspects of the intrusion of a unified series of events upon their lives, Pan-Indigenous experience is beginning to make sense, on a global scale, of the events of the past several centuries. It is only now that the nature of this momentous series of events, by which the hegemony of one small continent was expanded to the rest of the world, is beginning to be understood.

It should be the goal not only of the emergent Indigenous pan-globalism but of the world at large, including those whose ancestors were instrumental in achieving this expansion, to begin the process of understanding fully the implications and consequences of the historical era that is now coming to a conclusion. In the end, it will only be by such a critical revaluation of the past that the present can come to be understood.

The root problems created by the domination of one cultural paradigm over another are at the very heart of the Indigenous experience of the world today. Until the core concerns are dealt with, the common symptoms of contact, conflict, and crisis will remain. Until the common threads of intrusion are identified, examined, and compared there can be no attempt at a reweaving of the cloth of which Indigenous societies are formed.

Commonalty of historical circumstance has united Indigenous Peoples in common purpose. When this experience can be understood, and the knowledge of the healing process pioneered and shared, then through time and only time can the process of reconstruction begin. This is a road down which the survivors must travel by themselves, aided by the efforts of fellow travellers. Yet this road to renewed cultural awareness, self-identification, and vitality, and this process of cooperation along the new path taken is the inevitable culmination of past and present events for all Indigenous Peoples who hope to survive into the unknown worlds of the future.

CHAPTER 4

FUTURE

PROSPECTS FOR THE FUTURE

With one foot planted firmly in the traditions of the past, and one foot placed partly in the present, all Indigenous societies today find themselves in a world that is filled with a host of seemingly irreconcilable opposites. All such societies must now either forge a new and hybridized set of societal values with the strength to persevere against the assault of the dominant society, or be totally assimilated within it.

For most Indigenous societies the viability of the traditional ways of life exists now only in the collective memory of the elders. Contact with the dominant societies among which they live has eroded the need for many traditional aspects of life, rendering them redundant. No Indigenous society has remained immune to the effects of catastrophic change imposed upon its traditional lifeworld. No Indigenous society anywhere in the world has retained the entirety of its traditional way of life into the present. Nowhere today does any traditional economy of any Indigenous People exist that is viable in its entirety.

Without a complete suite of perceptual and conceptual tools, randomness, disorder, and seeming chaos have come to characterize Indigenous perceptions of a world they once knew and fully understood. Indigenous Peoples everywhere have had to come to the profound realization that many of their traditional tools fail to interpret the reality of the present. There is no going back. The past cannot be resurrected. It exists only in memory now.

Faced with a fractured past, Indigenous Peoples must also come to terms with an ill-understood present. This presents a double difficulty. While members of the dominant society have had many generations to internalize the necessary accommodations that this system requires in order to achieve a modicum of success within it, Indigenous Peoples have not. Achieving any measure of accommodation requires the forging of a whole new set of societal values, and places fundamental traditions at great risk. Solving this dichotomy is difficult indeed.

For the dominant society, whose core values have evolved to corre-

49

spond to the demands of the economic system within which they live, success within that system does not require any seemingly contradictory compromises. For Indigenous Peoples it does: in many cases the demands of the industrialized economy run directly counter to their traditional beliefs and values. The present industrial world economy is not their system, yet they find they are forced to make difficult decisions and compromises to it and within it, for which, cognitively and conceptually, they are not fully prepared. For Indigenous Peoples, the industrialized world remains an externally imposed reality, not yet fully internalized.

Even if accommodation is made to some aspects of this external economic reality, Indigenous Peoples find that they are marginalized within it. This is the double difficulty: forced by necessity to accommodate to the realities of an alien environment, they are not allowed to participate fully within it. Racism and discrimination exist on many levels, and have become concrete realities for all Indigenous Peoples today. Easily identifiable as racial and ethnic minorities, Indigenous Peoples find they are not welcomed as full participants in the dominant societies of which they are now expected to become a part. They find themselves profoundly isolated from a mainstream that has consistently failed to accommodate them.

Caught between competing versions of separate worlds, Indigenous Peoples must now choose paths for the future. There are still many Indigenous societies in the world today with the strength to unite their members into cohesive cultural identities. All face the same inevitable choices in the long term. In the face of overwhelming change, all must either create new realities or lose their identities as unique societies.

All cultures experience continual change. Rapid and unrelenting change can threaten the very heart of a culture, and place its continued existence in jeopardy. Some, perhaps most, Indigenous cultures will inevitably disappear from the face of the earth. Rendered redundant by the march of "progress," many are doomed. However, some Indigenous cultures will survive, and some will thrive. Resiliency in the face of change is the hallmark of cultural strength. Many Indigenous societies, such as the Inuit of the Arctic and the Mapuche of Chile, have proven themselves marvelously adaptive in the past. Many have begun the process of creating new cultural identities by preserving core values from the past and marrying them with the realities of the present in order to synthesize viable entities with which to meet the demands of the future.

For there to be a future for Indigenous societies, there must be a basic and fundamental need for those societies to continue to exist. There must exist a cultural coherence that is able to adapt to the new world. There must be a strong and expressed desire to bring cultural values from the old world into the new, and to meet the demands this new world will inevitably impose.

The new world of the future is one in which seemingly irreconcilable differences in cultural perspectives must be reconciled in ways that are compatible to both Indigenous and industrial societies. Dichotomies exist, and their resolution will be the true test of resiliency for all Native societies. There is a need to assemble solutions that, when tested in the crucible of a harsh reality, are found to be both sustainable and sustaining in a changing world.

Out of the reconciliation of opposites will emerge new Indigenous cultural identities. These frameworks are being set in place today. Indigenous Peoples are now discovering that they do indeed have the power to affect changes in their own lives. All over the world Indigenous Peoples are reaffirming their abilities to determine their own futures in their own ways.

THE NATURE OF DICHOTOMIES

The intrusion of industrial time and space has now forced the many disparate cultures of Indigenous Peoples to make a series of choices. In all areas of the world Indigenous People must now choose between various aspects of competing paradigms. In a broad range of areas associated with culture, political organization, economics, and associated philosophies and cosmologies, Indigenous Peoples, collectively and individually, must now make a whole suite of choices based upon competing aspects of traditional and industrial ways.

Many decisions will have to be made between old ways of life ill remembered and new ways not yet assimilated or fully perceived. Circumstances conspire to force choices for which Indigenous Peoples may not be fully prepared. Often these choices are made without a full knowledge of their consequences, both intended and unintended, or without a full knowledge of their ultimate impact or repercussions upon Indigenous societies. Yet these difficult decisions must be made. How they are made, in what order, and in what magnitude is of vital importance to Indigenous societies today, and will characterize these societies in the future.

These decisions of what to retain and what to abandon from the traditional, and what to adopt or reject from the modern industrial intrusions, are being made on three levels. On the individual level, every

Aboriginal person today is faced with a spectrum of choices, and faces great pressure to make these choices wisely. Often these choices are mutually exclusive. For example, to obtain the formal education required to enter employment within the dominant society, it is often necessary to do so exclusively in the manner and custom of the dominant society, and at the expense of time spent learning the traditional cultural discourse and language. The acceptance of wage employment may preclude participation in the traditional economy. To become a member of the religion of the dominant society, one may have to forswear the religious beliefs of one's ancestors in whole or in part.

On a family level, where a great deal of the strength of traditional Indigenous societies still lies, the collection of individual decisions must somehow be rationalized into a cohesive unit allied by blood ties. Often Indigenous families today exhibit a panoply of the manifestations of such decisions throughout the generations. It is not uncommon to find Indigenous households in which the grandparents retain the traditional lifeworlds relatively intact, while the younger children live in a new world set apart, an electronic space age. It is often the case that grandparents and grandchildren are unilingual in different languages, uniperceptual in differing concepts of time and space. Often they can no longer communicate with each other.

The sum of these individual and family decisions is the societal reality of Indigenous Peoples today. In most such unbuffered societies, the encroaching time and space of external reality have intruded beyond collective control. The individualism of modernity is now assailing traditional ties, one individual decision at a time. A wind is but a collection of moving molecules driven by an external force. Everywhere, and at all levels, the global winds of change are blowing over Indigenous Peoples today.

A COMPARISON OF INDIGENOUS AND INDUSTRIAL DICHOTOMIES

The following columns give some indication of the broad range of decisions Indigenous Peoples have faced in the past, or face today. These broad categories are a distillation of the menu that contact with the now-dominant world culture has thrust in front of them. Though necessarily generalized, and in many cases oversimplified and condensed into words and phrases that represent abstractions of complex concepts, the nature of these dichotomies and the core value judgments they entail are familiar territory to Indigenous Peoples anywhere.

52

By selecting some items from column A, some from column B, and by ignoring those that have no relevance, these societies have in essence unconsciously created, or are creating, new and in some cases hybridized cultural combinations.

This game is compulsory: contact immediately signals inception. The stakes are high, the rules are alien, and the cards are marked, yet Indigenous Peoples cannot choose not to play. The resolution of seemingly irreconcilable opposites on any one issue is difficult, and often involves considerable compromise. Compromise negates absolutes: for Indigenous societies an arbitrated draw is often the only possible outcome.

A representation of some of these dichotomies is listed below under the headings of "Industrial" and "Indigenous," and represent abstractions of two sides of the same coin. In all cases the industrial version of the dichotomy represents the world of modernity as portrayed by an industrialized and essentially Eurocentric society. The Indigenous version represents preindustrial society as incorporated in representative Aboriginal precontact societies. In all cases generalizations are made in an attempt to portray the broad range of choices that Indigenous societies face as a result of continuous contact with an expansionist world of industrial modernity and its associated metanarratives.

A—Industrial	*B—Indigenous*
•money as "capital"	•nature as "capital"
•quantitative	•qualitative
•domination of nature	•living within nature
•large-scale economic projects that are concentrated	•small-scale economic projects that are spread out
•centralization	•decentralization
•individual creativity is often subverted	•individual creativity is encouraged
•democratic or autocratic decision-making	•consensus decision-making
•alienation from the processes of government on a day-to-day level	•active participation in the processes of government on a day-to-day level
•power concentrated in the hands of a few	•power broadly based in the hands of many
•strong ethic of direct leadership	•strong ethic of collective leadership

◆"economics" as a separate and specialized area best left to "experts"	◆"economics" as inseparable from other aspects of daily life
◆dehumanization of work	◆humanization of work
◆workers leave home to travel to a work site	◆workers work close to home
◆work alienates worker from family	◆work is performed in family units
◆work emphasizes material gain	◆work emphasizes spiritual gain
◆individual ownership	◆collective ownership
◆concern with goods	◆concern with services
◆work is provided by an external provider	◆work is evident, not provided
◆work is assigned	◆work is selected
◆work is time allocated	◆work is task allocated
◆strict control of time	◆flexible time
◆hours, minutes, days	◆seasons
◆linear time	◆concentric time
◆leisure as an alternative to work (rest time)	◆work and leisure as part of the same process
◆ethic of competition	◆ethic of cooperation
◆work-related stresses	◆stress associated with external variables
◆resources at a distance	◆resources close at hand
◆urban focus	◆rural focus
◆mobility of labor	◆immobility of labor
◆capital intensive	◆labor intensive
◆economic rigidity	◆economic adaptation
◆elimination of perceived obstacles to economic "progress"	◆willingness to accommodate to changes in economic circumstances
◆land/means of production can be owned individually	◆land/means of production are held collectively
◆legal titles and deeds can be held individually	◆no such concept
◆exclusivity of lands is on a personal level and enforced by legal strictures of society	◆exclusivity is cultural and enforced by force, one culture to another, but not within cultures
◆limits to land and territory are	◆lands are demarcated only by

demarcated by manmade monuments

- land is an "economic" resource like any other
- land belongs to "us"
- one major model of economic organization
- economic success is measured quantitively
- success measured by accumulation
- economic specialization
- profound belief that economic change can be imposed from outside a society

- structures of society are formalized and rigid
- formal education away from home
- "teachers" are outsiders away from home
- ethic of individualism
- actions reflect upon an individual
- permanent institutions
- eccentricity is generally not tolerated
- deviance is punished by confinement within society
- problems are isolated away from society in general
- parameters of society are at a large supranational level
- coalitions of interests expand to form broad segments of larger societies
- ability to form large and coherent large-scale interest groups

natural and preexisting boundaries

- land is the source of life
- "we" belong to the land
- many models of economic organization
- economic success is measured qualitatively
- success measured by peer review
- economic generalization
- profound belief that economic change can only be accomplished from within a society

- structures of society are flexible and implied
- informal education at home
- "teachers" are family members at home
- ethic of "kin-ism"
- actions reflect upon a kin or clan group
- fluidity of institutions
- eccentricity is generally tolerated
- deviance is punished by exile from society
- problems are dealt with at a community level
- parameters of society are at a localized level
- ranges of interests are at a local or culture-wide level of self-interest
- great differences and intertribal enmities are difficult to overcome

✦literate traditions	✦oral traditions
✦preservation of details	✦preservation of concepts
✦monotheism	✦pantheism
✦structured religious dogma	✦unstructured and fluid animism
✦primarily male deities	✦male and female deities
✦concepts of "god" as "above" earth	✦concepts of "god" as "in" and inherently part of the earth.

This list could easily be expanded, and would eventually grow to include nearly all aspects of daily life for all Indigenous Peoples. Faced with this daunting array of choices, all Indigenous societies are presently reformulating their cultural parameters and creating new versions of reality in the face of overriding needs to do so. Wherever these adjustments lead, from wholesale retention of traditional values to outright assimilation, Indigenous Peoples the world over are faced with a situation in which they now must respond to these external challenges, the consequences of which penetrate to the very core of their existence.

CONCLUSION

All Indigenous societies today have been irrevocably altered by contact with a dominant world economy based upon capitalist industrial exploitation and its associated metaphysical underpinnings. All have faced, and continue to face, daunting challenges and choices in their quest to absorb what they perceive to be the best of what this new world has to offer, while struggling to retain that which they value from the traditional ways of life. New, altered, and hybridized cultures are emerging from this process.

These emergent lifeworlds are neither "traditional" cultures in the true sense of the concept, not are they truly part of the new world order, and most will never be. The present is a time when these hybrid cultures are being tested and refined. Experimentation, and finding out what works in this "real" world, now characterizes Indigenous lifeworlds, as the readjustments are being firmed into the cultures that will carry Indigenous Peoples into the future.

What will this future hold for Indigenous Peoples? What is it that Indigenous Peoples want from the dominant societies in which they now live? What are the basic demands these newly emergent Indigenous entities are beginning to articulate?

First and foremost, all Indigenous Peoples desire the opportunity to survive. At the very basic level, all Indigenous Peoples value those things they share as a culture, those commonalties that set them apart from all other peoples. All Indigenous societies want, at a minimum, a chance to hand down those core identifying values they hold dear to succeeding generations, in their own ways and without interference.

All over the world, the dominant perceptions of reality are being challenged by a rebirth of Indigenous pride and a renewal of self-worth. Estrangement is giving way to accommodation to the modern society. New concepts and philosophical constructs are now being incorporated into the Indigenous "tool-box" of ideas. Indigenous Peoples are finding solutions that work. All over the world Indigenous Peoples are saying loudly: "We are here, we cannot be destroyed, and we will be here forever."

At the local, national, and international levels a host of new Indigenous organizations dedicated to rekindling cultural pride have emerged in recent years. Non-governmental organizations (NGOs), such as Indigenous Survival International and the World Council of Indigenous Peoples, have secured intervenor status in various forums and are attempting to coordinate efforts on a global basis. Pan-Inuit associations such as the Inuit Circumpolar Conference are actively involved in many facets of international cooperation. National groups are emerging in most nations with Indigenous populations, and are beginning to have an effect on governmental policy in some jurisdictions. As well, there are now a host of non-governmental organizations, such as the Workgroup for Indigenous Peoples, based in Holland, which are organizing to support these nascent efforts.

On a worldwide basis this can be seen to be a movement. This movement represents a profound realization by Indigenous Peoples everywhere that their traditional lifeworlds are in grave danger of disappearing. The choice has been made abundantly clear: Indigenous Peoples must either consolidate what they value now, or face total assimilation.

The growth of vibrant Aboriginal organizations dedicated to cultural survival in the face of these challenges has come to characterize the Indigenous experience of the latter years of the twentieth century. Most Indigenous societies have proven to be remarkably resilient in the face of a host of external threats to their existence. Faced with the forced alteration or removal of many aspects of their traditional lifeworlds, Indigenous Peoples have had to learn to cope with massive and unrelenting change as a constant fact of life.

Many Indigenous Peoples have moved from the Stone Age to the atomic age and beyond within the span of a single human lifetime, and have had to internalize and incorporate ideas and ideals of new realities at or near the very margins of perceptual abilities. There are Indigenous People alive today who can both craft stone tools and operate a facsimile machine.

The steady winds of change have propelled the dominant societies to a standard of living unparalleled in human existence. These changes were accomplished as an uninterrupted series of subtle sea-breezes, one following upon the other, through which it has been possible for the dominant society to gain their sea-legs gradually, and to seek an equilibrium and isostasy moderated by the passage of time. Indigenous Peoples have not had the benefit of generations of adaptive time: they have been swamped by the passage of a sudden surge of unrelenting change, which has flooded over them like a tidal wave. They are only now beginning to right themselves from this onslaught, and to seek isostasy, to regain their rightful place in the new world order that now surrounds them.

Throughout the changes that have engulfed them, all Indigenous societies have managed to retain certain core values central to their existence. Outward accommodation can be, and in many cases has been, accomplished without alteration of the essentials that constitute the essence of Indigenous being. While many Indigenous Peoples may now wear jeans and work in wage-labor jobs, and drive automobiles or fly in airplanes, they remain, at their very core, Indigenous. Most are now building upon these core values in a concerted effort to reformulate their collective identities as distinct peoples, and to translate these into the resolution of the primary dichotomy that all Indigenous Peoples face today: the role in which tradition can be reconciled in a modern world of change.

Within this world two forms of accommodation are being reached. All Indigenous societies have had to accommodate to new and altered patterns of existence, and are restructuring their lives accordingly. The internal strength that they are developing, the cultural pride that is now emerging, and the empowerment occasionally evident, are the necessary series of constructs that are needed to ensure continued cultural survival.

Not only must Indigenous Peoples accommodate themselves to the larger society, they must, through their newfound organizational identities, find acceptable ways to ensure that the dominant society will accommodate to them. This will be a difficult task. It is only now being initiated. In order to even secure a voice with which to articulate their demands for accommodation within the power structures of the dominant society, Indigenous Peoples will have to learn a whole new way of

58

speaking. They must somehow convince the dominant societies in which they live to allow them space, in all of its aspects and forms, in order to continue to live and continue to develop as separate cultural entities.

It is somewhat ironic that Indigenous Peoples must first compromise and accommodate to the dominant systems in which they live before they can even begin to argue to that system that it should begin to accommodate to their concerns. Yet this is what has happened, and what is happening today.

In all nations in which Indigenous Peoples now live, there are bright, educated, and articulate Indigenous individuals who have managed to successfully straddle the gap between both worlds, and who can present to the dominant society, in ways that they can understand, a rationally reasoned argument for accommodation. It is somehow ironic that Indigenous Peoples, who previously existed without a legal profession, are now beginning to hire, or indeed become, lawyers to pursue their demands, to successfully argue with the ethics of the dominant system against itself for their own ends and purposes.

Indigenous Peoples are discovering that there is a power that comes from within a vibrant and resurgent culture, and they are now attempting to organize to assert that power in new and novel ways. In a world awash with change, new versions of old societies are emerging everywhere. Precedent molded through use into pattern need not necessarily be endlessly repeated.

Indigenous Peoples everywhere are not only reestablishing and redefining themselves, but are articulating the parameters of the new societies they are creating, and are beginning to defend these identified perceptual borders against the continued intrusion of the dominant societies that now surround them. Indigenous Peoples are actively seeking realignments of power.

All Indigenous societies have now begun to voice their concerns. Not only are they seeking a form of accommodation from society at large, they are now demanding, in an organized and increasingly effective way and in the name of international justice, certain inherent rights from within the dominant societies in which they live.

In essence, after the specifics have been distilled, most Indigenous desires and demands can be condensed into three basic requests for accommodation.

First, a secure and tenured land base, approximating as far as is possible the extent of the territories that have been alienated from them. Indigenous Peoples are connected to the land in spiritual ways that are difficult for non-Indigenous people to fathom. Without such lands on which to live and secure a livelihood, assimilation is inevitable. All Indigenous groups are willing to accept that there are competing interests in the lands they claim. Most are willing to negotiate.

Second, the desire for a viable and culturally relevant economy based on a mixture of traditional and sustainable renewable resources with non-traditional developments of their own choosing, and incorporating a community-oriented approach to economic development. Indigenous Peoples are not opposed to all development, only to those aspects that are destructive to their cultures. Given the appropriate conditions, they are willing to share resources with the dominant societies, providing there are perceived benefits for both sides.

Third, the right to a measure of political self-determination as distinct peoples; the ability to organize to preserve valued cultural traditions; the ability to say no to outside forces and interests; and the ability to make their own mistakes in their own way in all relevant aspects of their life as they themselves determine them.

There are a host of decisions to be made by Indigenous Peoples today between seemingly irreconcilable opposites that must somehow be reconciled. Faced with a common affront to their existence, Indigenous Peoples worldwide have now begun to consolidate with common cause. They are beginning to coalesce on common fronts, to unite on many levels in mutual purpose, and to share amongst themselves the many commonalties and realities of Indigenous experience.

The learning curve this has entailed has been that of an alien culture, and it has been exceedingly steep. Yet it is beginning to be ascended. The tides of change have flowed over all Indigenous societies everywhere. The alien economy and its legion metaphysical supports has intruded upon all aspects of all traditional Indigenous lifeworlds. The Indigenous 4 percent of the world's population, however, have now begun to find the will to voice their concerns loudly, and have begun to demand, in the name of humanity and justice, a meaningful place as nations in their own right on the national and international stages. Their voices are beginning to be heard.

BIBLIOGRAPHY

Armstrong, R., Kennedy, J., & Oberle, P. R. 1990. *University education and economic well-being: Indian achievement and prospects.* Ottawa: Indian and Northern Affairs, Canada.

Arndt, H. W. 1987. *Economic development: The history of an idea.* Chicago & London: The University of Chicago Press.

Australian Bureau of Statistics. 1990. *Aboriginal People in the Northern Territory.* Darwin: Government Printer of the Northern Territory.

Beauclerk, J., Nerby, J., & Townshend, J. 1988. *Indigenous Peoples: A fieldguide for development.* New York: Oxfam.

Berger, T. R. 1991. *A long and terrible shadow: White values, Native rights in the Americas: 1492–1992.* Vancouver & Toronto: Douglas & McIntyre.

Berger, T. R., ed. 1989. *The Arctic: Choices for peace and security.* West Vancouver: Gordon Soules.

Berger, T. R. 1988. *Northern frontier, northern homeland: The report of the Mackenzie Valley Pipeline Inquiry* (rev. ed.). Canada: Minister of Supply and Services.

Berger, T. R. 1985. *Village journey: The report of the Alaska Native Review Commission.* New York: Hill & Wang.

Berger, T. R. 1981. *Fragile freedoms.* Toronto: Clarke, Irwin.

Berger, T. R. 1980. *Report of Advisory Commission on Indian and Inuit Health Consultation.* Ottawa: Department of Supply and Services.

Bethell, L., ed. 1984. *Cambridge history of Latin America.* Cambridge: Cambridge University Press.

Bodley, J. H., ed. 1988. *Tribal peoples and development issues: A global overview.* Mountain View, CA: Mayfield.

Branford, S., & Glock, O. 1985. *The last frontier.* London: Zed Books.

Brosted, J., et al. 1985. *Power: The quest for autonomy and nationhood of Indigenous Peoples.* Bergen: Universitets Forlaget.

Brundtland, G. H., Chair. 1987. *Our common future: The report of the World Commission on Environment and Development.* Oxford & New York: Oxford University Press.

Burger, J. 1990. *The Gaia atlas of First Peoples: A future for the Indigenous world.* New York: Anchor Books.

Burger, J. 1987. *Report from the frontier: The state of the world's Indigenous Peoples.* London & New Jersey: Zed Books.

Byers, R. B., & Slack, M., eds. 1986. *Strategy and the Arctic.* Toronto: Canadian Institute of Strategic Studies.

Chamberlin, J. E. 1975. *The harrowing of Eden: White attitudes toward North American Natives.* Toronto: Fitzhenry & Whiteside.

Churchill, W. 1985. The situation of the Indigenous populations in the United States. *Akwesasne Notes, 17*(1), 18–19.

Clark, B. 1990. *Native liberty-Crown sovereignty: The existing Aboriginal right of self government in Canada.* Montreal & Kingston: McGill-Queens University Press.

Clay, J. 1988. *Indigenous Peoples and tropical forests: Models of land use and management from Latin America.* Boston, MA: Cultural Survival.

Cobo, J. M. n.d. *Study of the problem of discrimination against Indigenous populations.* UNESCO: Commission on Human Rights, Ch. 11.

Connolly, B., & Anderson, R. 1987. *First contact: New Guinea's highlanders encounter the outside world.* London: Penguin Books.

Davis, S. 1977. *Victims of the miracle: Development and the Indians of Brazil.* Cambridge, MA: Cambridge University Press.

de Vos, G., & Wetherall, W. 1983. *Japan's minorities.* U.N.: Minority Rights Group, Report No. 3.

Diaz, B. 1975. *The conquest of New Spain,* Cohen, J. M., trans. London: Butler and Tanner.

Eberhard, W. 1982. *China's minorities: Yesterday and today.* California: Wadsworth.

Friede, J., & Keene, B. 1971. *Bartholome de Las Casas in history: Toward an understanding of the man and his work.* Dekalb, IL: Northern Illinois University Press.

Gibson, C. 1964. *Aztecs under Spanish rule: A history of the Indians of the Valley of Mexico, 1519–1810.* Stanford: Stanford University Press.

Gillmor, D. 1992, March. Chief Justice: Ovide Mercredi. *Saturday Night.*

Goehring, B., & Stager, J. 1991, November. The intrusion of industrial time and space into the Inuit lifeworld. *Environment and Behavior, 23*(6), 666–680.

Goldsmith, E., & Hildyard, N. 1984. *The social and environmental effect of large dams.* London: Wadebridge Ecological Centre.

Government of India. 1990. *Report of the Commissioner for Scheduled Castes and Scheduled Tribes,* yearly annual. New Delhi: India.

Gray, A. 1987. *The Amerindians of South America.* New York: United Nations, Minority Rights Group.

Hall, S. 1987. *The fourth world: The heritage of the Arctic and its destruction.* London: The Bodley Head.

Hanke, L. 1974. *All mankind is one: A study of the disputation between Bartholome de Las Casas and Juan Gines de Sepulveda on the religious and intellectual capacity of the American Indians.* Dekalb, IL: Northern Illinois University Press.

Hanke, L. 1959. *Aristotle and the American Indians.* Chicago: Henry Regnery.

Harris, R. C., ed. 1987. *Historical atlas of Canada: Volume 1. From the beginning to 1800.* Toronto: University of Toronto Press.

Hemming, J. 1970. *The Conquest of the Incas.* London: Macmillan.

Hopper, J. H., ed. 1967. *Indians of Brazil in the twentieth century.* Washington, D.C.: University of Washington Press.

Bibliography

Hunter, R., & Calohoo, R. 1991. *Occupied Canada: A young white man discovers his unsuspected past.* Toronto: McClelland & Stewart.

Jones, S. 1978, January. Tribal underdevelopment in India. *Development and Change,* 9(1), 41–70.

Jull, P., & Roberts, S., eds. 1991. *The challenge of northern regions.* Darwin, NT: Australian National University.

Las Casas, Bartolome de. 1971. *History of the Indies,* Collard, A. M., ed. and trans. New York: Harper Torchbooks.

Lineton, P. 1978. Soviet nationality policy in northwestern Siberia. *Development and Change, 9,* 87-102.

Little Bear, L. 1976, December. A concept of Native title. *CASNP Bulletin,* pp. 58–62.

Livingstone, I., ed. 1982. *Approaches to development studies.* Aldershot, Hampshire, England: Gower Publishing.

Macdonald, R. 1989. *The Maori of Aoteroa-New Zealand.* New York: United Nations, Minority Rights Group.

McNeill, W. H. 1976. *Plagues and peoples.* Garden City, New York: Anchor Books.

Materne, Y., ed. 1980. *The Indian awakening in Latin America.* New York: Friendship Press.

Miller, J. R. 1989. *Skyscrapers hide the heavens: A history of Indian-White relations in Canada.* Toronto: University of Toronto Press.

Moody, R., ed. 1988. *The Indigenous voice,* (Vols. 1 & 2). London & New Jersey, Zed Press.

Morse, B. W. 1991. *Aboriginal Peoples and the law.* Ottawa: Carleton University Press.

Myers, N. 1985. *The primary source: Tropical forests and our future.* New York: W.W. Norton.

Nash, M., ed. 1977. Essays on economic development and cultural change. *Economic Development and Cultural Change, 25,* Supplement.

Nikiforuk, A. 1991. *The fourth horseman: A short history of epidemics, plagues, famine and other scourges.* Toronto: Penguin.

Ortiz, R. D. 1984. *Indians of the Americas.* London: Zed Press.

Paine, R. 1982. *Dam a river, damn a people.* IWGIA Document No. 45. New York: United Nations.

Patterson, E. P. II. 1972. *The Canadian Indian: A history since 1500.* Don Mills: Collier-Macmillan.

Ramenofsky, A. F. 1987. *Vectors of death: The archeology of European contact.* Albuquerque: University of New Mexico Press.

Reynolds, H. 1982. *The other side of the frontier.* Harmondsworth: Penguin.

Ribiero, D. 1970, trans. 1970. *Indian civilization.* Rio de Janiero: Brasiliera.

Ridington, R. 1990. *Little bit know something: Stories in a language of anthropology.* Vancouver & Toronto: Douglas & McIntyre.

Ridington, R. 1988. *Trail to heaven: Knowledge and narrative in a northern Native community.* Vancouver & Toronto: Douglas & McIntyre.

Ridington, R. 1983. From artifice to artifact: Stages in the industrialization of a northern Native community. *Journal of Canadian Studies, 18*(3), 55–66.

Ridington, R., 1982. Technology, world view and adaptive strategy in a northern hunting society. *Canadian Review of Sociology and Anthropology, 19*(4), 469–481.

Roberts, J. 1981. *Massacres to mining: The colonisation of Aboriginal Australia.* Victoria: Dove Communications.

Rose, C. M. 1985. Possession as the origin of property. *The University of Chicago Law Review, 52*(73), 73–88.

Rowley, C. D. 1988. *Recovery: The politics of Aboriginal reform.* New York: Penguin.

Sahagun, Bernardino de. 1989. *Conquest of New Spain* (1585 revision), Cline, H. F., trans. Salt Lake City: University of Utah Press.

Sauer, C. 1932. *The Road to Cibola.* Berkely: University of California Press.

Shah, G. 1984. *Economic differentiations and tribal identity.* Delhi: Ajanta Publications.

Schumacher, E. F. 1976. *Small is beautiful: A study of economics as if people mattered.* Tiptree, Essex: Anchor Press.

Tennant, P. 1990. *Aboriginal peoples and politics: The Indian land question in British Columbia 1849–1989.* Vancouver: The University of British Columbia Press.

Tolan, S., & Postero, N. 1992, February 22. Accidents of history. *The New York Times Magazine.*

Trigger, B. 1985. *Natives and newcomers: Canada's 'heroic age' reconsidered.* Montreal & Kingston: McGill-Queens University Press.

United Nations. n.d. *Covenants 107 & 169 concerning Indigenous Peoples.* New York: International Labour Organization.

United Nations. n.d. *Preliminary report on the study of discrimination against Indigenous populations.* UNESCO: Commission on Human Rights.

United Nations. 1985. *Rights of Indigenous Peoples to the earth.* Geneva: World Council of Indigenous Peoples, Commission on Human Rights.

United Nations. 1982, August. *Bonded labour in India.* U.N.: Sub-Commission on Prevention of Discrimination and Protection of Minorities.

Valkeapaa, N.-A. 1983. *Greetings from Lappland: The Sami: Europe's forgotten people.* London: Zed Press.

Vitoria, Francisco de. 1991. *Political writings,* Pagden, A., & Lawrance, J., eds. Cambridge: Cambridge University Press.

Wenzel, G. 1991. *Animal rights, human rights: Ecology, economy and ideology in the Canadian Arctic.* Toronto: University of Toronto Press.

Williams, B. W. n.d. *The passage of Maori Land into Pakeha ownership: A Maori view.* Christchurch, New Zealand: Cabbage Tree Publications.

World Bank. 1992. *Tribal peoples and economic development: human ecological considerations.* Washington: World Bank.

World Bank. 1991. *World data and statistics.* U.N.: World Bank, Annual.

Wright, R. 1992. *Stolen continents: The 'New World' through Indian eyes since 1492.* Toronto: Viking.

INDEX

Aborigenes (Australia), 7, 17, 33, 34, 41
Africa: and change, 2; distribution of Indigenous Peoples in, 6, 8; Eritreans, 43
Ainu (Japan), 33
Amazon Basin. *See* Brazil
Amehusha (South America), 33
Aracanian Indians (Argentina and Chile), 20
Arctic: and borders, 3; and change, 2; resiliency of peoples, 50
Argentina, 20
Aristotle, 25, 27
Asia: distribution of Indigenous Peoples in, 6, 8; past occupation of, 9. *See also* individual countries
Atomic weapons. *See* Nuclear testing
Aztec Empire, 13, 17, 25
Australia: distribution of Indigenous Peoples in, 7; economic discrimination, 33; loss of Indigenous populations in, 17; mineral reserves, 41; mortality rates, 34; unemployment in, 34
Bali. *See* Indonesia
Bangladesh: armed struggles in, 43; resettlement programs, 39
Battle of the Little Big Horn, 20
Bhil (India), 41
Bhilalas (India), 41
Black Death, 11
Blackfoot (North America), 8
Bolivia: distribution of Indigenous Peoples in, 7; loss of Indigenous populations in, 17
Borders, 3–4, 7, 23, 42
Brazil: dams, 41; destruction of rainforests in, 40; economic discrimination, 33; education, 34; gold in, 42; loss of Indigenous populations in, 17, 35; mortality rates, 34; resettlement programs, 39. *See also* South America
Burma. *See* Myanmar
California. *See* North America
Canada, 4; dams, 41; economic discrimination, 33; education, 34; distribution of Indigenous Peoples in, 7, 8; mineral wealth, 42;

unemployment in, 34; urbanization, 38. *See also* North America
Capitalism, 22; adaptation to, 16; dependence on, 45–46; expansion of, 1, 20; extent of, 10, 15, 37; profit motive, 10, 11
Caribbean Islands (Carib Indians), 16, 24
Central America: loss of Indigenous populations in, 17. *See also* individual countries
Chakma (Bangladesh), 41
Charles V of Spain, 25
Chile, 20; resiliency of peoples, 50
China: distribution of Indigenous Peoples in, 6; nuclear testing in, 44; resettlement programs, 39
Christianity, 11, 26–27
Colombia: coal, 42
Columbus, Christopher, 11
Cortes, Hernando, 13, 17
Crown lands, 24
Custer, General George A., 20
Dams, 40–41
Dandami (India), 41
de Las Casas, Bartholome, 26–27
de Sepulveda, Juan Gines, 25–26
de Vitoria, Francisco, 27–28
Dene (Arctic), 3
Denmark, 7
Dichotomies, 51–56
Dominica. *See* Caribbean Islands
Ecuador: loss of Indigenous populations in, 17
Enlightenment, 30
Ethiopia: armed struggles in, 43
Eritreans (Africa), 43
Europe: Age of Discovery, 12, 24; alliances with Indigenous Peoples, 13, 30; conflicts with Indigenous Peoples, 19; distribution of Indigenous Peoples in, 6, 8; extermination of Indigenous Peoples, 13, 24; fifteenth-century, 10–14; rationalization of new world acquisitions, 25–26; relationship to land, 22; rights of first discovery, 23–24, 27; settlement of new worlds, 14, 29; technological advances in,

12, 18, 19, 25; urbanization of, 38. *See also* Scandinavia
Fiji, 7
Fourth World, 5
French Polynesia: distribution of Indigenous Populations in, 7; nuclear testing in, 44
Frontiers, 39, 42
Fulani (Africa), 8
Garimpieros, 42
George III of England, 31
Greenland. *See* Kalaallit Nunaat
Guajiro Indians (Colombia), 42
Guam, 7
Guatemala: armed struggles in, 43; destruction of rainforests in, 40; distribution of Indigenous Peoples in, 7; education, 34; mortality rates, 34
Haiti, 13
Inca, 13, 17, 25
India: armed struggles in, 43; dams, 41; destruction of rainforests in, 40; distribution of Indigenous Peoples in, 6; economic discrimination in, 33; and education, 34; iron ore in, 42
Indian Wars of the American West, 20
Indigenous economies: definition of, 1; development of, 14; future, 60; systems, 21; threats to, 38
Indigenous lifeworlds, 2, 36, 46, 47, 56; definition of, 15; destruction through depopulation, 18
Indigenous Peoples: alliances with Europeans, 13, 30; and capitalism, 16, 45–46; and change, 1–3, 9, 15, 36, 45, 47, 50, 58; and choices, 51–56; classification of, 4, 47; commonality, 46, 47, 48, 57; conflicts with Europeans, 19; demoralization of, 17, 25, 37; discovered by Europeans, 23–24; displacement of, 39; economic discrimination against, 33; and education, 34; and epidemics, 16–17; European extermination of, 13; 24; government departments for, 37; marginalization

Publisher's Note

Purich's Aboriginal Issues Series

Welcome to the first book in this series. After two decades working with Aboriginal Peoples and issues as Director of the University of Saskatchewan Native Law Centre, a legal aid lawyer, an author, and a university lecturer, it is clear to me that there is a great need for well written and researched materials on Aboriginal issues. This series is intended to fill that gap and to help non-Aboriginal people gain an appreciation of Aboriginal aspirations. I hope these books will fill that need by being available as teaching and reference tools.

This book provides an introduction to the world's Indigenous Peoples. Other books currently in progress will deal with self-government, Inuit cultural perspectives, and the Aboriginal history of the Cypress Hills area. Additional titles will follow.

Donald Purich, Publisher

About Purich Publishing

Purich Publishing, founded in 1992, specializes in materials on Aboriginal, agricultural and legal subjects for the educational, research, legal, and reference market. Inquiries from authors are welcome.

NOW AVAILABLE

Law, Agriculture and the Farm Crisis $28.35

This 160-page book examines issues such as farm debt, GATT, farm subsidy programs, environmental regulation and the development of farm policy. Edited by law professors Ken Norman and Donald E. Buckingham, the book includes contributions from lawyers, agricultural economists, and psychologists from both Canada and the USA. The price includes $3.50 for shipping and $1.85 for GST.

Fax your order to **(306) 373-5315** or order by mail from:
Purich Publishing
Box 23032, Market Mall Postal Outlet
Saskatoon, SK Canada   S7J 5H3
or through your bookstore.

—